Open to Glory

Renewing Worship in the Congregation

Carol Doran
Thomas H. Troeger

Judson Press ® Valley Forge

OPEN TO GLORY
Second Printing, 1993
Copyright © 1983
Judson Press, Valley Forge, PA 19482-0851

The Scripture quotations contained herein are from the New Revised
Standard Version of the Bible, copyrighted 1989 by the Division of
Christian Education of the National Council of the Churches of Christ in
the United States of America, and are used by permission. All rights
reserved.

Library of Congress Cataloging in Publication Data

Doran, Carol.
   1. Public worship. 2. Liturgics. I. Troeger,
Thomas H., 1945-   . II. Title.
BV15.D67 1983 264   82-18753
ISBN 0-8170-0981-7

Printed in the U.S.A.

Photograph on page 14 supplied by
The Metropolitan Museum of Art.
Bequest of Mrs. H. O. Havemeyer, 1929.
The H. O. Havemeyer Collection (29.107.18)

For every faithful soul

open to glory

and

especially those

whose stories fill this book

Contents

Chapters

Open to Glory

New Possibilities for Worship

Worship leaders from more than twenty congregations had met with us for two days. We had shared dozens of new ways to sing and pray and preach. Yet by the conclusion of the conference something more important than any single method had emerged. A pastor summarized what he had learned in these candid words: "A friend of mine asked why I was coming to this worship workshop. 'You have been leading services for thirty-eight years; don't you know all you need to know by now?' In one sense my friend was right. I have been praying, preaching, baptizing, and serving the Lord's Supper all of these years, and, to be honest, I was not exactly sure what I wanted when I came here. I only knew something was missing from our church's worship though I could not name it. But now I can. It came clear to me yesterday. When we shared our different images of God, I realized how limited my own had become. I want to know more of the fullness of God. I want to be more open to glory, and I want that for my people when we gather to worship."

The pastor sat back in his chair, and the other ministers and lay leaders nodded their heads in agreement. The pastor's honest confession captured the primary insight which had illumined our time together.

Open to glory.

That is the core of this book: how worship opens us to the glory of God. There are plenty of suggestions about what you can do with services, but if you speed through these pages looking for this idea or that for Sunday morning, you are going to miss out on the greater possibilities for worship. You will manage to find new material to enliven your services, but the methods will fade and falter if they are not related to a larger process of understanding your church as a community of God's people. That is why we urge you to take your time with this book and to read it with your worship committee or the ruling board or the church staff, for the revitalization of worship which we outline here depends on a community that is on a journey of faith, exploring deeper and further and higher the reality of God.

We begin by asking you to identify the qualities of God that are expressed and celebrated in your weekly services. What does your worship reveal about God? What does it hide? Without such reflection you will not appreciate the riches and strengths of who you already are as a church. You may experiment with ideas that are not appropriate to your congregation's identity or style of worship. Many attempts at innovative worship fail because they utilize ideas that have not grown out of the tradition or faith-experience of the community. Most ministers can give testimonials to the truth of this. They move to a different church and try something that soared in the last congregation but falls flat in the new setting.

Revitalizing worship begins then with an exploration of who God is *for your worshiping community.* That last phrase is crucial. You may be tempted to assume that it is perfectly clear who God is. The Bible, the church, and, above all, Jesus Christ have made manifest who God is. Yes, they have. But in working with hundreds of churches and with seminary students from dozens of traditions, we have discovered that even though people claim one Lord, one faith, one baptism, they carry strikingly different understandings of their relationship to God into the sanctuary.

Some congregations enter their churches in silence, expressing the awe and solemnity which they feel before God. Other congregations enter chatting and looking around at everyone to see who is there. They are responding to their sense of God's presence in the friendly warmth of the fellowship.

Some congregations sit perfectly still in their pews, their bodies mirroring the stillness of a soul listening for the eternal word. Other congregations sway and clap their hands, their motions set loose by waves of the Spirit rolling among them.

Some congregations meet in churches filled with visual symbols to suggest the inexhaustible riches of divine meaning. Others gather in plain churches that witness to the clean, clear truth of God.

Some congregations sing hymns with a steady beat and predictable chords which stress the logic and structure of the Creator. Others sing foot-stomping, heart-warming tunes that celebrate Jesus, the personal Savior.

Obviously what brings life and joy in one church may seem awkward and misplaced in another. Yet even within a single congregation there is a greater variety of understanding than usually finds expression in corporate worship. That is bound to be the case whenever a group of individuals gathers together, but it has become even truer in recent years. Pastors in workshops tell us again and again that their congregations are more heterogeneous than in the past, that it is not uncommon to find several traditions represented in a church even though it bears a particular denominational name. Naturally enough, people bring to worship memories of their earlier church background—favorite hymns, treasured rituals, beloved prayers, and readings. These different traditions are ways to know "more of the fullness of God," to become "more open to glory." But in most congregations they go untapped because the worship leaders realize how tender the sensibilities of the dominant tradition are when it comes to changing anything in worship.

Jack Curl, a priest in Walker Percy's novel *The Second Coming,* knows this fear of changing the form of services: "He had been terrified that Marion, who had found him through her search committee and who considered the interim prayer book an abomination, would fire him."[1] "Terrified" is not too strong a word as any innovative worship leader can tell you. We must not pretend this fear does not exist, for it is connected to something much greater than opposition to a new hymn or a different style of prayer or a revised format for the Lord's Supper. In a world whose foundations are shifting and shaking, people seek a stable center for their lives, and one major way to find that center is in services of worship that are dependably the same. Resistance to change in worship comes in part from a profound human need to know that there is enduring truth, an everlasting reality which is not only talked about but which also is ritually embodied week after week. Peter Berger helps us understand this need when he describes the *nomos* or meaningful world order which religious communities supply.[2] The members of the community make sense out of their lives by placing their joys and tragedies under the larger constellations of divine meaning that are provided by their tradition. And nowhere in a church's life are these constellations more visible than in the worship of the congregation. When we ask people to pray or sing to God in a new way, we are asking them to modify their structures of sacred meaning; and that can touch off a vehement response, one which is seemingly out of proportion to what we have introduced.

Max Frisch's parable, *Man in the Holocene*, provides an image that is helpful in grasping the anxious character of the contemporary soul trying to maintain a world of order and meaning against disruptive forces.[3] Herr Geiser, the central character, arranges all that he knows by writing information on sheets of paper, cutting pages out of the encyclopedia, and tacking and taping these scraps to the walls of his living room. The papers keep falling on the floor, and in the end they all come down in a heap. Sunday's worshipers have known a similar collapse of meaning in their daily lives. The patchwork of ideas with which they have papered the walls of their craniums keeps coming down, and when people step into the sanctuary, the last thing they want to sense is that the same chaos reigns inside the church. How we order our worship involves nothing less than the care of the human soul, broken and anxious and eager for enduring truth.[4]

Effective change in worship must be related to a dependable pattern of meaning, to some fundamental theological understanding. "I want to know more of the fullness of God," said the minister at the workshop. "I want to be more open to glory, and I want that for my people when we gather to worship." Here is the basis of worship reform, not to shake the soul that already wobbles, but to strengthen the soul with an expanded vision of the glory and wonder of God. When worship embraces more of who God is, we discover more of who God made us to be and more of what God wants us to do. We do not mistake the constricted limits of private meaning for the perimeters of holy truth. We find ourselves willing to consider a variety of approaches to God that have been present but hidden in our congregation.

When our differences find appropriate expression in corporate worship, the doors of the church open and heaven's fresh breezes blow through the congregation. Note the metaphor: breezes. It suggests wind, Spirit, change. It is different from our earlier image of constellations of meaning which imply constancy, reliability, familiarity. Our starting assumption is that like sailors at sea our churches need both—constellations to guide us and breezes to drive us. If we keep only to our fixed patterns of meaning—same hymns, same prayers, same rituals—our worship stalls in the doldrums. Or if we follow only the blowing of change—new hymns, new prayers, new rituals—we end up "tossed to and fro and blown about by every wind of doctrine, by people's trickery, by their craftiness in deceitful scheming" (Ephesians 4:14). Therefore, as we begin our voyage, we assure people that we shall rely on both the wind of the Spirit and the constellations of meaning which have guided us in the past.

Jesus has a beautiful expression for the comprehensive vision which needs to be a part of revitalizing worship. "'Therefore every scribe who has been trained for the kingdom of heaven is like the master of a household who brings out of his treasure what is new and what is old" (Matthew 13:52). The reformation of our worship can be seen as a way of training for the kingdom of heaven, a way of probing through the storehouse of Scripture, tradition, history, and art and discovering both new and old treasures. Some treasures will be familiar while others will be brand new. Or they may be ancient but new to us because they have been neglected for so long. Often a church is unaware of the extraordinary richness of its past, and what it thinks of as new or even revolutionary represents in fact the reclaiming of a tradition that was lost. For example, the high degree of congregational responsibility for worship which we stress in this book is not at all new. As we shall see in chapter 3, it has roots that reach back to Scripture and to the early church, and it was vigorously renewed by the free church tradition during the seventeenth century, only to be lost once again in the revivals of the 1800s.

Whatever way you envision the revitalization of your church's worship, as a voyage or as training for the kingdom, it is essential that the change you make be a faithful expression of the community's belief and experience. All worship needs theological integrity, a fundamental coherence between what we believe and what we do when we gather before God as a congregation. In our work with churches we have discovered five principles which can help congregations evaluate the theological integrity of their services.

1. *Worship must be faithful to the Word of God.* We have deliberately stated this "Word of God" and not simply "the Bible" because, as central as the Bible is to Christian worship, we do not worship the Bible. Rather, we worship the living Word, the One through whom all things were created. The Bible is the "canon," the "measure" of faith by which we test our belief and probe our experience. But to name something the measure of faith is not to declare it the boundary of faith. So we ask of our worship: Are we faithful to the living Word who addresses us in the pages of Scripture and the history of our traditions and meets us here and now?

2. *Worship must be in touch with the roots from which it has sprung.* It is not a matter of saying word for word and doing act for act what our forebears did. That would be deadly. But we need to maintain our corporate memories so that we do not lose our

sense of identity. Communities that forget their past, like individuals suffering amnesia, do not know who they are in the present.

3. *Worship must be expressive of contemporary experience.* This does not mean bowing to every fad and whim of popular culture. Rather, it suggests the need to be connected to the vital events, rhythms, and questions which mark people's lives and which they bring into the sanctuary. Worship does not deny the raw experience of daily life. It illumines the hidden dimensions of that experience and enables us to return to the workaday world alive to the sacred presence in common things.

4. *Worship must engage the fullness of our humanity.* God made us whole beings, feeling as well as thinking, seeing as well as hearing, physical as well as spiritual. Worship that engages the entire person in the praise of God is more faithful to the Creator who made us heart and soul, mind and body.

5. *Worship must include all members of the community.* It is easy for worship leaders and worship committees to pattern services according to the limits of their own experience, thus excluding others who may attend out of loyalty but who do not feel part of the community. The last three decades, like the opening of the church to the Gentiles in the first century A.D., have revealed an increasing awareness that God's family is not limited by race or gender or ability. Including the full human community in the words and actions of worship witnesses to the God who made and loves all people.

To follow these principles of theological integrity in developing a church's worship services is to practice a spiritual discipline. It involves listening to God while we examine the most profound issues of a congregation's faith and life together. Worship leaders who practice this discipline with an appropriate committee or board will discover that the Spirit has wondrous things to say to the church and that the congregation can in fact become more open to the fullness of God, more open to glory.

How Does the Congregation See Christ?

Understanding the Community

No two worshipers view Christ in exactly the same way. Like the figures in the Rembrandt etching to the left, each member of the congregation looks from a particular vantage point, and each assumes a posture expressive of how he or she is related to Christ.[1] Some are in bright light, close and intent upon the gospel. Others blend into the shadows or listen from the periphery of the crowd. Yet all of them are in the picture and in our congregations, too.

We invite people at our workshops to step into Rembrandt's scene, to identify with the character who most nearly represents their perspective and posture in the presence of Christ. During an opening service we help people locate themselves in the crowd by sharing our fantasies about four of the characters. The visual and dramatic experience calls on people's imaginations as well as their logic. It engages the whole human being which we described under our principles of theological integrity. Thus the process of evaluation and reformation not only talks about new possibilities for worship, but it also lets people taste them.

15

Stepping into the picture clarifies people's relationship to Christ while it expands their sensitivity to the varieties of belief, doubt, and seeking that are present in a congregation. It helps them understand what is happening during worship for the entire community, not only for themselves but also for people who share a similar perspective and posture.

Where are you in the picture?

Are you the figure standing in the back right corner, wearing a floppy hat, your arms crossed as you pull your coat about you, perhaps thinking impatiently:

That preacher's taken my place.
I usually beg where he's standing.
It's a good spot,
farmers setting up fruit stands,
merchants laying out their wares,
tourists with lots of loose change.

I wish the preacher would get it over with.
I don't put much stock in religion.
You can't make supper from a sermon.
Maybe you're like me.
Maybe you'd rather stand in the back corner,
listening in but not moving close to the center.

I'm always wondering about the stuff preachers preach about:
Is it real?
Coins in my hand
—that's real.
Steak and potatoes on my plate
—that's real.
But the love that passes all understanding
—well?
I never knew that love when I was growing up.
That's why I left.
I told my folks to give me whatever money I had coming.
They did.
Mom wept and Dad stared at the ground.
I couldn't tell if they were angry or sad.
Seemed they were both at the same time.

The money went.
I'd just as soon not talk about it.
Fact is it's gone so doesn't matter how.

I thought once I might go home.
I never did though.
Just been doing odd jobs and begging ever since.
Some days I get my share,
especially when my spot's not taken by some preacher.
Then I go to a restaurant and order a full meal—
appetizer, drinks, main course,
and whatever's chocolate.
All the time I'm eating, I'm looking at the tables around me,
families telling the younger ones to sit up,
business men laughing over their wine,
young couples holding hands,
and all the time I'm wondering about the laughter and the
    loving.
Is it real?

Then I get up and walk back to the room I rent.
Sometimes in the dark on my bed
I go back home.
The folks are dead now.
The place has been sold for years.
But I picture them the day I left,
Mom weeping, Dad looking down,
and I call out,
"It's me.
Can I come home?"
And sometimes in the silence,
I swear it's true,
I hear a voice.
It's Mom's voice, Dad's voice,
close but distant, familiar but strange,
"I've been waiting for you all these years."
Then my stomach growls.
My tongue rubs the last thin taste of chocolate from my mouth.
I roll over, trying to get comfortable.

And I wonder,
Is it real?[2]

Do you make room for this character in your congregation's
worship, a place for the yearning soul who listens from where
the edges of doubt and belief overlap? The worship of God flows
from glad, abundant faith; and the church does not design
services to feed people's skepticism. But any congregation that
wants to share the gospel must have an opening, a space in its
worship which, like the gate in the background of Rembrandt's
picture, beckons the seeking soul toward Christ. There needs
to be a prayer or a period of silence or a piece of music or a
ritual or a word of assurance that invites and welcomes those
who find themselves not yet ready to step toward the center,
who have faith no greater than a mustard seed.

It may be that, from where you are in the picture, you cannot
even see the figure standing in the background. Perhaps you
are the man in the stocking cap whose right elbow rests on the
corner of the platform and whose hand covers his mouth and
chin while his eyes gaze into the distance, as if the truth he is
listening to comes from beyond his usual world:

I said I would do all that I've done.
And I did.
I said I would finish at the head of my class.
And I did.
I said I would take a job in the firm
and work my way to the top.
And I did.
I said I would marry and start a family
once my career was sure.
And I did.
There's the youngest one,
Jacob,
next to me in my wife's arms.
The boy just beyond,
doodling during the sermon,
that's Jake's older brother.
He's a little slow.

But this younger one is going to follow me.
Jake is going to make something of himself.

"There was a man who had two sons;
and the younger of them said to his father,
'Father,
give me the share of property that falls to me.'
And he divided his living between them.
Not many days later,
the younger son gathered all he had
and took his journey into a far country,
and there he squandered his property in loose living."

Squandered it all?
If you ever pull something like that on me, Jake,
don't come crying back to me.
Don't come back asking me to help you out.
Because I won't.

"I will arise and go to my father,
and I will say to him,
'Father,
I have sinned against heaven and before you;
I am no longer worthy to be called your son;
treat me as one of your hired servants.'"

Don't try that line on me, Jake.
Don't think smooth words can make up for hard work.
Don't think I'll give in to rehearsed excuses.
Because I won't.

"But the father said to his servants,
'Bring quickly the best robe,
and put it on him;
and put a ring on his hand,
and shoes on his feet;
and bring the fatted calf and kill it,
and let us eat and make merry;
for this my son was dead, and is alive again;
he was lost, and is found.'"

Dead?

Jake—dead?
But alive again?
Alive?
Oh, give me my child.
Give me my living child.
I'll love him and love him and love him.
I will.[3]

Do your worship services allow time for God's grace to penetrate the heart of the legalist?[4] Or is there such busyness to your worship, one thing immediately following the other, that the service contradicts the message of the gospel? That can easily happen. Our anxiety to have everything go in order sometimes pulls us into a pattern of marching lockstep through our ritual. We end up embodying an image of Christ which confirms the rigidity and self-righteousness of the graceless soul.

Perhaps you are harder to spot than the figure in the floppy hat or the man whose hand covers his chin, because you are nearly swallowed in the darkness behind Jesus' raised right hand.

I stand in the shadow
because I am afraid to see Christ face to face.
I call him "Teacher,"
but not yet "Lord."
I like his stories
because they're the way life is:
children running off from home,
then coming back sorry,
some of the family wanting to make them pay the price,
but the parents are just glad to know they're alive.
Love and jealousy,
anger and forgiveness,
grace and grudges
—all tangled together—
that's the way life is.
I've watched people.
That's how I know.

I've watched people
coming up to him after he's done.
They walk right up
and look him square in the face.
It happened the other night,
with that woman down front who's holding the child.
She came close with him in her arms and said,
"Lord,"
and before she got any further,
he blessed the child.
The way the woman smiled,
you knew that's what she wanted.
I was ready then
to step around front and say,
"Lord,"
but the crowd didn't give me room.
I pulled back in the shadows,
waiting my turn to speak.
It never came,
and I walked home alone.

But I'm back today,
still in the shadows,
yet hoping the others will give me a chance to say,
"Lord."[5]

Will this person get a chance through your church's worship
to make that commitment? Or to reclaim a commitment made
long ago that now is faded and worn? Worship which proceeds
Sunday after Sunday without providing a symbolic way to re-
vitalize the loyalties of the heart ignores a profound pastoral
need. Some weeks that occasion may be as simple as a hymn
of dedication or words of exhortation to those intending to lead
a new life, but other times it may take more dramatic form, from
church-wide covenant renewal—not uncommon in the free
churches of New England during the seventeenth century[6]—to
a ritual for the remembrance of our baptisms.

William H. Willimon records a moving story in which a pastor,
after leading a woman through a ritual of baptismal renewal,

asked if others would like to renew their vows. The entire
congregation stood up![7] They were moving as one body toward
the center of faith, taking their places with the woman who sits
next to Jesus in Rembrandt's picture, her left cheek resting on
her left hand. Perhaps she averts her eyes from the others
because she is thinking:

I overhead someone say,
"Pushy woman,"
when I sat down at Jesus' feet.
I know it's the place of honor for a rabbi's students,
a place reserved for men.
But whatever anybody else says,
he welcomes me.

When I tell people,
"Jesus saves,"
they ask,
"Are you the woman taken in adul—?"
Then they catch themselves,
embarrassed,
and I have to finish the sentence for them,
"The woman taken in adultery?
No, I'm not.
Though I've seen her at these meetings.
You can pick her out by the strength in her eyes."

And I'm not the woman who met Jesus at the well either
—I've been asked that too.

Jesus saves
by asking me to use my mind.
He saves me again and again
from assumptions and roles which,
to be honest,
I fall for as easily as those who ask,
"Are you the woman . . .?"
Jesus saves
not because Jesus is the answer
but because Jesus is the question.

My Lord and Savior calls into question
all the little systems of thought and custom
that clip the wings of the soaring heart
and silence the rhapsodic soul
and stifle the probing mind.
I leave these gatherings
free
from what the world says
must be,
free
for what God says
will be.[8]

When the benediction is pronounced and the postlude sounds
in your church, do people leave with a vision of glory to remind
them of what God says will be? Consider more than the sermon
in answering this question. We believe in the power of preaching, but sometimes the sermon does not break through as effectively as a phrase that lifts a need to heaven in corporate
prayer or a hymn whose rhythm sends people out to the beat
of the Spirit or a bulletin cover with a scene which, like the one
we have just explored, serves as a visual parable, an icon of
faith that mirrors the struggles of a believing, seeking community.

We need to consider the worship service in its entirety. We
need to give as much attention to its composition as Rembrandt
gave to his etching. Note what holds the picture together, what
gathers persons in the congregation out of their diverse worlds.
It is a single figure: Jesus Christ. The artist has formed the
picture so our eyes move to the middle. He has not left anyone
out. The skeptic in the floppy hat is as much a part of the scene
as the believer at Christ's feet. Yet the focal point is clear. What
Rembrandt has done in his etching is what we must do in our
worship—provide room for the whole crowd but keep the focus
on the center.

Does your service do that?

Think of worship as a feast given by a gracious Host who has
promised to supply the most important things—Spirit, strength,

mercy, faith, hope, love—but who has left the details to you. Every service is a meal, because even when bread and wine are not served, we still gather to feed on God's Word. The Host is depending on you to take care of the table arrangements, to help people feel welcome, and to set the tone for the whole celebration. Here is a list of items to review:

Consider the music you have chosen.

Look at the setting in which you gather.

Note how you sit, stand, and move.

Feel the mood and pace of the worship leadership.

Examine the bulletin you hand people.

Ask if your language captures the joy and awe of the occasion. That is a lot to think about at one time! So we will go through these items in more detail, always mindful of this question: Have we provided room for the whole crowd while keeping the focus on the One who calls us together?

How Christ Is Portrayed Through Music

Rembrandt's etching is perceived as light and dark areas on a flat surface. The eye sees nothing more than this, but the mind and heart find such fullness of meaning in this graphic representation that we can almost hear the figures speaking. We provide our own soundtrack for the etching.

How else could this scene become real for us? Except for those whose hearing is impaired, a significant part of human experience is the sea of sound in which we live. Our minds automatically recall the times we have been in large groups of people. Occasional sounds of movement as people try to find a more comfortable position or ease a cramped limb, children dropping the toys given them for quiet play, whispering and mumbled discussion among pairs here and there—all these are to be expected. We are reminded of how like the people in the etching we are. We have a growing sense of being present as our Lord is teaching.

Sound is part of our own congregation's picture. Like life itself, it is present but unseen. Our ears gather vast amounts of information out of thin air, and our brains process and cause our bodies to respond to it even while we are conversing or reading a book. How mysterious is the means by which the characteristic sound of a familiar voice is heard and recognized; how fitting that God's people should have discovered and savored and perpetuated the use of sound to give glory to their Creator!

Sound affects us deeply, even when we do not consciously listen to it or intentionally interpret its message. Most people are equipped from birth with auditory sensors that discern instantly how loud or quiet a sound is, how high or low, how simple and clear or how rich in coloration of tone. Alteration of any one of the many characteristics of sound is noticed by us. We are naturally sensitive to sound as message and signal. When the level of sound at the coffee hour following a Sunday service is abruptly increased or decreased, we are immediately attentive to the change. "What was that?" we ask of those around us, or, "What's happening?" A sudden crash or an eerie calm sets off an unconscious alarm system within us even before we consciously consider what might have caused it.

If random sound is able to communicate so many clear messages to us, consider the glorious possibilities of music, which is organized sound. In music the highs, lows, louds, quiets, colors, and duration of sound are all marshaled into service. The limitless possibilities of all their arrangements and combinations draw from our memories and spark our imaginations. Even though these messages may never find their way into words, we sense their meanings and our inner response is involuntary.

There is no universal pattern of sound which symbolizes Christ, no melodic theme which all can interpret as the Christ motif. When our Lord is present through hymns and choir and instrumental music in our churches, it is by varied and diverse means, not all of which involve sound.

Congregational hymns form the largest body of church music with which contemporary Christians have regular involvement. In hymns, Christ is portrayed through both the words and the music. The specific pairing is important. When a text about God's authority in the universe is coupled to a strong tune with sturdy harmonic progressions and steady accompaniment, the text's message is reinforced. The nave and the people singing are filled with a single resounding message.

While the text and tune of each hymn should proclaim a unified message, use of only one kind of hymn in community worship portrays a Christ of limited dimensions. God is truly worthy of praise and is also the One to whom we cry in times of trial. We sing thanks to God and we remember the sacrifice made for us on the cross. If our song centers only on the image of God most precious to the worship leaders, we are neglecting an easily accessible source of renewal for the entire congregation.

Hymn singing is an expression of our church's corporate life. Our singing together portrays the Christ among us. Music gives form and beauty to the words, which in turn draw people into the text. Seldom does a congregation's responsive reading equal its hymn singing for sheer enthusiasm.

What is the dominant theme of the hymns sung in your church?

You can find clear and useful information about your present use of hymnody by looking back over copies of the past year's bulletins. Is the theme God's presence in the world around us or the transcendent God? Sometimes the hymns center on our sinful nature, sometimes on Jesus as Savior and Lord. We need a healthy mix of all that is theologically appropriate to our congregation. The distinct theme of each service also should be apparent. Hymns old and new should appear. We believe that the living God continues to inspire hymn writers in our time.

Everyone enjoys the old tunes, but it is important to introduce new music to the congregation from time to time. Worship leaders usually have clear, even biblically based reasons for their choices: "This ancient tune from our tradition reflects the highest musical quality. Nothing less is fit for the praise of God." Or "This new tune is exciting. It reminds us that God is present in our world."

Sometimes we forget that introducing the new tune, no matter what its merits, includes thoughtful planning of the congregation's pastoral needs. People's first impression of a new tune or the words sung to it is often overshadowed by feelings of being excluded from the singing, of frustration, and of anger.

We reflect the image of Christ in our churches by recognizing the needs of our people for musical preparation and assistance in accepting new things. A brief spoken introduction at a scheduled time before the worship begins will help prepare them to sing a new hymn with confidence when it is part of the worship service.

Choirs form a special category. They are part of, but in some ways apart from, the congregation. In all that they do they have opportunity to portray Christ to the congregation and to grow in grace as they use their special gifts.

Like the hymns, the choir music must sing out the message of God's presence and power and of all that the gospel holds for us. The manner in which the music is presented is as important as the specific selection sung. The sight of the choir and how members act as individuals and in relation to one another in the group send a message to those watching and listening.

Consider, too, the instruments used in our services and why we use them, for music's spirit may be enhanced or crippled by the choices we make. Scripture does not favor one musical instrument over another, but earnest and colorful debates on the subject fill library shelves and continue to rage in the twentieth century. Often it is assumed that the instruments conventionally used in our own experience are the only ones appropriate for use in any church in any century. Do we imagine that God is better pleased by this instrument or that? Could we believe that God would be displeased at a specific instrument's praise? The rejection of songs and offerings in the fifth chapter of Amos was purely on the basis of accompanying sin, not because of the harps or the songs themselves.

It is obvious that some instruments are better suited than others for the size of the congregation and for the music they are singing at any given moment. Accompanying and descanting instruments should be chosen on the basis of availability of skilled players, the condition of the instrument itself, and its appropriateness to the music being used.

If instruments, which are mentioned in the Bible, are the source of controversy in our churches, how much more do we debate the matter of musical style, which is not discussed in

Scripture? An acquaintance once asked whether we used traditional or contemporary music in our seminary chapel. The question implied that naming one category or the other would provide a full description of our community's "style."

The choice of music for worship is like other artistic choices. It is not easily described by outlining limitations. That is not the nature of art. We have said we seek to portray Christ in what we sing and play on our instruments. Several aspects of these hymns and anthems and instrumental music must be considered, but "style" is not one of them.

First and above all stands the question of the music's quality. Within its own framework of musical practice, does it qualify as "very good" or, preferably, "excellent"? We sometimes forget that the music of many significant composers of past generations varied in quality even though the style may have been consistent. Most of the less inspired material, mercifully, has not survived, but if it had, we would not be justified in presenting it in our churches simply because it had come from the pen of a great musician. Our portrait of Christ may be presented in a contemporary style or in a manner valued in centuries past, but it may not be of poor quality.

We must ask ourselves another question about music being considered: Is this an honest expression of faith? And further, does every honest expression of faith deserve the congregation's time and attention just for being itself? Some honest musical efforts simply are not interesting or uplifting.

There will be occasional situations when the church may wish to hear the less sophisticated compositions of its members, and there will be many more times when compositions written by musicians who profess non-faith will be sung or played in church. In the latter instance we judge that God is singing through the work of this musician whether the human instrument is attentive to the message or not.

We have come to central questions for those leading Christian worship: How shall we determine and maintain the musical standards which are important and beneficial to the spirit and health of our community? How shall we avoid succumbing to the temptation of adopting an arbitrary standard, one which we believe others outside our congregation expect us to maintain or one we would choose if the music were our worship alone?

The community's music does not belong to us. The worship we lead is the work of the people. The praise is sung by and for all of us. It is the people's task and their privilege to collaborate in planning congregational worship, and it is our task and privilege as leaders prayerfully to guide and enrich that process.

How Christ Is Portrayed Through the Setting and Actions of Worship

What do worshipers see from the pews in your sanctuary?

The answers to this question are no more self-evident than the answers about how music functions in your service. Most of us only know what we see from the particular pew we take Sunday after Sunday. But what about the people who sit far behind us or off to the side or near the organ console or up in the balcony? What do they see? Remember the Rembrandt picture, each character looking from a particular vantage point, some close and intent upon the gospel, others listening from the edges. To see how the rest of the congregation sees the service, you need to stand where others stand; you need to sit where others sit.

One of the most common mistakes in examining worship is to assume that it is purely a matter of word and thought. We know of a church that announced this constricted understanding in its bulletin: "Worship is thinking right ideas about God." Perhaps, but worship is much more than thinking. Faithful worship engages the whole human being whom God created—heart, soul, and body as well as mind. When we worship, we do not think songs. We sing them, breathing air into our lungs and returning it to heaven, mixed with sounds of praise. We do not think prayers. We pray them, bowing our heads or standing or kneeling as "sighs too deep for words" (Romans 8:26) stream out of us. We do not think about Christ feeding us. We are fed, tasting bread and wine at our lips while love and grace pour into our hearts. Furthermore, we sing, bow, stand, pray, and eat together in a special room that represents for many people a universe of meaning and memory. Perhaps it is where we first acknowledged to others that "Jesus is Lord" or where we promised ourselves to another "for better for worse, for richer for poorer, in sickness and in health as long as we both shall live" or where we listened to the words "ashes to ashes, dust to dust" spoken over our best friend or where quite simply week in and week out we renew our strength to face whatever life demands.

Because worship is more than thinking right ideas about God, because it is the embodied action of a particular congregation in a particular space, we need to base our discussion on more than theoretical considerations. For example, a worship committee considering "how to build a greater sense of community" may find that there are sharply different perspectives on the amount of congregational involvement already present in the service. Some of the debate will stem from different concepts about worship. But another significant source of conflict may be traced to where people usually sit during the service. Those who are close to the pulpit and table may feel an intensity of engagement that simply is not possible for the choir sitting in a loft at the back of the sanctuary.

Therefore, the first step in understanding your church's worship is not to discuss it around a table in a room where you never hold services. Go into the sanctuary with your entire worship committee. Let each person take a place different from the one he or she usually occupies on Sundays. If you usually sit in the balcony, take a pew on the main floor. If you normally sit in the back pew, take the position of the worship leader in the chancel. If you sit up front, sit in the rear. If on the side, sit in the middle.

Look slowly around you.
Slowly!
What do you see from your new location?
Name it.
Describe it.
Tell what meaning it has for you.
What do you not see that you usually see?
What members of the congregation are in your field of vision?
Who is not?

Do you feel more a part of the community in your new location?

Less?

If you are a worship leader and used to viewing all the faces of the people, you may be quite disoriented by sitting in a rear pew, seeing nothing but the backs of people's heads. Or if you take the position of worship leader for the first time, you may be surprised to see all those faces looking at you. We highlight this contrast because it is often a source of different perceptions about what happens in a service. Many worship leaders experience the congregation's individual and corporate personality because nearly all the time they are seeing faces mirror the joy, sadness, burden, thanks, boredom, or praise of the community. At the same time, there are people in pews whose lines of sight encourage a highly privatized experience of worship. That may be precisely why people take a particular spot week after week. They are listening from the periphery, not ready to move toward the center, or they consider worship to be a highly solitary act even though it takes place in community.

But many worshipers would welcome a view that would pull them more completely into the action of the service. We think of a church where the choir is hidden by a wall to the right of the chancel. They cannot see the congregation, and the congregation cannot see them, except when they come out and gather behind the Lord's table to sing their anthem. However, throughout the service people in the pews see choir heads peeking around the wall to get a glimpse of the congregation. What splendid worshipers those choir members are! They realize that worship is a community event and that to be part of it they must see as well as hear. Those faces out in the pews represent nothing less than the body of Christ, and it is Christ whom people have come to church to see and know.

If you have never given this much thought to your worship setting, you may at first be put off by so much attention to detail. What matters most is that people worship God in spirit and truth (John 4:23-24), not in the front pew or the back pew, not in the chancel or the choir loft. God looks at the heart. Right!

But the setting in which we place ourselves can have a profound impact on the posture of the soul. Our interior state is not easily separated from our surroundings. Think of what trouble you will go to in arranging a dinner party for your best friends: linen, china, silver, a center piece, maybe even placecards. You want it to look good as well as taste good. You know that the appearance and the way things are served will be as important as remembering to put a dash of nutmeg in the dumplings. Surely we should take equal care in preparing Christ's feast. We have been invited to eat with the One who set stars blazing in the heavens, knit together our bones, died for us, stole away the power of death. A diplomatic feast bringing together the president of the United States and the premier of Russia is nothing compared to what happens when two or three gather together in the name of Christ. Guess who's coming to dinner at your church. Does the place look the way you want it to?

It may be that you cannot rearrange the space in your sanctuary or that you will not want to, but at the very least you need to be aware how your setting influences your worship. For example, a long, narrow sanctuary offers different possibilities from a squarer space in which pews or chairs encircle the Lord's table. Sometimes people return from a workshop eager to try a style of worship that delighted them in the new setting, but when they do, the service does not feel right in their home sanctuary. What fits in one space does not fit another. If you invite me over to eat pizza in your kitchen, my attire and behavior will be different from that on an evening we spend in your dining room eating from your best dishes. The setting matters. Any discussion about worship that proceeds merely at the level of thought is not dealing with the full reality of what is involved when the congregation gathers together. Worship leaders must never be content asking, "Is that a good idea for a service?" They must ask as well, "How will that look, sound, and feel in our particular church?"

We cannot think about the space in which we worship without also considering how we move and act. While your worship committee members are positioned in their new places in the sanctuary, hand them all a bulletin for a service in which you celebrate the Lord's Supper. Let your worship leaders go through the service with you, being sure to walk, stand, or sit according to the usual custom. Do not rush through this exercise. Remember you are trying to get a sense of the entire congregation's experience, not just your own. Your new location can alert you to details you never thought about before.

Consider, for example, the reading of Scripture, an action common to nearly every Christian tradition which connects us to the synagogue worship in which Christ himself participated. Note how the spatial and visual characteristics of your sanctuary frame the hearing of God's Word. First of all, from where does the reader have to walk? Is there a microphone wire on the floor or are there narrow steps which are difficult to negotiate and which make the reader's body tense? During this period of time members of the congregation are preparing to hear God's Holy Word—unless instead they are worrying that the person will stumble on the way forward. Where do you want the congregation to pour its spiritual energy: into anxiety about the reader or in getting ready to receive God's Word?

From what kind of Bible is the Scripture read? Does the reader carry it forward or is it already in position? A ragged paperback version of The *Good News Bible* brought forward in a single hand suggests a less formal, more intimate understanding of God's Word. It gives the impression that the Word of God is something the reader shares out of his or her personal life. A large tome resting on the pulpit or table implies that the Word of God belongs to the entire community and the individual has been granted the privilege of reading from it on behalf of everyone. This latter understanding is stressed by the synagogue service in which Christ read. Luke describes in detail that Christ stood up, was handed the sacred book, and after reading from it, he returned it to the attendant and sat down (Luke 4:16-20). What do you want to stress in the reading of God's Word: that it is primarily a private word for the individual or that it is addressed to the entire community?

What forms the backdrop for the reading of the Word? We think here of a sanctuary which is three-fourths in the round. Viewed from one side of the church, the reader is framed by a deep blue stained-glass window that shows an angel delivering a scroll to a haloed figure on the ground. But viewed from the middle section, at right angles to the first perspective, the reader is outlined by a beige wall with an exposed speaker wire. That shift of ninety degrees gives a different feeling to the same action. Even those who do not keenly observe the details of their surroundings may be influenced at subliminal levels by what frames the reading of Scripture. What do you want to evoke in people when the Bible is read: the wonder and grace of God's communicating with us or the need to tend to the electrical system?

Can you see the reader's face from where you sit? Or does a light or microphone obscure your vision? Remember the hard of hearing who will be watching the reader's lips to complete through their eyes what is missed by their ears. And even those who hear well may be eager to catch that glance up from the page which signals the reader's awareness that these words are for everyone present.

Is the pulpit, lectern, or table too high or too low? If the reader looks uncomfortable standing there, a passage about God's grace will be contradicted by the gracelessness of an awkward posture.

Before the first word is out of the reader's mouth, these visual details set the tone for how the listeners will receive and respond to the Scripture. A hundred sermons on the importance of the Bible mean little if Sunday after Sunday we are sloppy about reading from it. The goal is not to be stagey or stilted but to embody in movement and posture the importance of what the congregation is about to hear. The worshipers should sense in the reading something of the awe which the psalmist feels for the ancient words of Israel:

> Give ear, O my people, to my teaching;
>   incline your ears to the words of my mouth.
> I will open my mouth in a parable;
>   I will utter dark sayings from of old,
> things that we have heard and known,
>   that our ancestors have told us.
> We will not hide them from their children;

we will tell to the coming generation
the glorious deeds of the LORD, and his might,
and the wonders that he has done.

(Psalm 78:1-4).

"Dark sayings from of old . . . the glorious deeds of the LORD."
Is at least a hint of the psalmist's wonder evoked by the reading
of Scripture in your service? If words are mumbled or are too
soft or too fast, there is no way that people can incline their ears
and hearts to God's dark sayings and glorious deeds. Here
again, sitting in a new location may be a revelation. Many
sanctuaries, including those with amplification systems, have
"dead" and "live" spots, places where the sound either gets lost
or is bright and clear. Sometimes hearing the Word of God hangs
on something as simple as changing where a reader stands or
redirecting the angle of a speaker.

We have focused on the reading from Scripture because it is
an action common to all of our worship traditions, but do not
limit yourself to that. Continue through your service using the
heightened awareness which we hope you have gained by now
to examine the other aspects of your worship. The comments
we have made about the posture, position, and movement of
worship leaders apply with equal force to every other part of
the service. For example, where a worship leader stands while
praying can influence how the congregation offers up the pe-
titions of their own hearts. A prayer spoken from the pulpit has
a different qualitative feeling from one offered among the pews
or from behind the Communion table. We know of a minister
who one Sunday walked halfway down the central aisle to offer
the prayers of pastoral concern instead of stepping into the
pulpit as was the usual custom. A dozen people later shared
how they had poured out their concerns to God as never before
during a service. A seemingly small action touched off a profound response in the congregation because it changed the spatial relationship between the minister and the people. The pulpit
in this particular church is placed at the front of the sanctuary,
above the people, a symbol of God's Word high and lifted up.
There certainly needs to be room for such an understanding in

our worship. But the elevated pulpit is a less precise symbol for the yearnings of the heart which arise from the congregation. They are more effectively represented by a prayer spoken from the same level as the people. The minister that morning used the space in the sanctuary to witness to the fullness of God, the God who is both beyond us (pulpit) yet very near (aisle). The minister was reclaiming the free church tradition of which his congregation was a part, a tradition in which the clergy preached from the pulpit but stood with the people to offer prayers. How accessible does God seem from where you lead the congregation's prayers?

How accessible does God seem in the way the Lord's Supper is arranged and served? Most of us have been to dinner parties where we never got to talk with the host because we were seated too far away or the table was arranged so our vision was obscured. We know a congregation where nearly a third of the worshipers could not see the breaking of the bread because the line of vision was blocked by the chancel railing. Those people who could not see had the feeling that a family of strangers was sharing a meal and passing the leftovers to them. Moving the table four feet forward so that its front edge was nearly even with the railings made it possible for everyone to feel included. Like the Rembrandt etching, this simple alteration provided room for the whole crowd while keeping the focus on the center of the gathering.

So far everything we have looked at involves the larger spatial relationship in the sanctuary. But this is only one aspect of our visual engagement during worship. The other is with the printed page—singing hymns, reading psalms and responses, offering up unison prayers. The movement of the eye from space to page involves a shift in the participants. Reading from a page is a more private act, requiring a different kind of mental operation which in turn influences the interior state of the worshiper, a fact which was recognized by the early English Baptist, John Smyth: "Reading sett formes of worship out of a book is quenching the Spirit . . . the matter is not brought out of the hart, but out of the book."[9] That is perhaps too radical a position for us, but there is truth in what Smyth says. It is easy to get lost in making sense out of the words that lie before us and thus to quench the Spirit.

Therefore, every congregational reading needs to be placed on the page in a way that minimizes our struggle with the words and maximizes our sense of worship. We have printed below the same unison prayer of confession in two different formats to give you a feeling for how much difference the layout can make in quenching or encouraging the Spirit:

Lord Christ, forgive us. We have seen you but not recognized you. Our eyes were blinded by doubt, by despair, by fear, by loneliness, by hate. Yet you were with us in the stranger, in the listening ear, in the kind word, in the shared meal. Open our eyes today. Prepare us to recognize you in the broken bread, in the people gathered around your table. And send us to tell the world: "The Lord has risen indeed." Amen.

Lord Christ, forgive us.
We have seen you but not recognized you.
Our eyes were blinded:
　By doubt.
　By despair.
　By fear.
　By loneliness.
　By hate.
Yet you were with us.
　In the stranger.
　In the listening ear.
　In the kind word.
　In the shared meal.
Open our eyes today.
Prepare us to recognize you.
　In the broken bread.
　In the cup poured out.
　In the people gathered around your table.
And send us to tell the world:
"The Lord has risen indeed." Amen.

The first format of the prayer requires more mental attention to keep one's place and to read along with everyone else. The second format has broken the prayer into simpler phrases so that the mind can give its energy to the Spirit rather than to the task of deciphering the meaning.

Consider your entire bulletin. How easy is it to find your way through the different parts of the service? Does the worship leadership give you enough time to make the shift from looking up to looking down and looking up again?

What is on the cover of the bulletin? Does it represent the gospel accurately? Think of the Rembrandt etching, a single picture rich with the truth of Christ and people's responses to him. There are endless possibilities for such visual parables of faith. Many churches have never developed them because of the commandment against idolatry. However, that commandment is directed only against making an image to which we bow down or serve. The worship of Israel involved the temple, the ark, the cherubim, altars, sacred books, and other symbols. When we do not think carefully about the visual expression of our faith, we end up marring our worship with images that are inappropriate or shoddy. Look again at your bulletin cover. Are you proud to present it to the Host of your church's feast as an emblem of his grace and love?

How Christ Is Portrayed Through the Words of Worship

Words strain,
Crack and sometimes break, under the burden,
Under the tension, slip, slide, perish,
Decay with imprecision, will not stay in place,
Will not stay still.[10]

What is true for the poet is true for the church. The words of worship keep slipping and sliding and decaying with imprecision. But unlike the poet, worship leaders can rely on more than language. We have seen how music, motion, space, postures, and symbols can give wings to words and fix their meaning in the heart. We have focused on these other aspects of worship not because worship needs to be a multimedia event, but because God's Word is not confined to speech. The Greek term for the divine Word is the *logos*, the root of our English suffix "logy" as in geology, biology, theology. The richness of the meaning of *logos* is simply lost in the English translation, "Word." The *logos* is the divine reality through which all things are created (John 1:3). Therefore, the visual and material aspects of worship witness along with our speech to the creative power of God's Word. The worship of most Protestant churches has not embodied this truth very completely, because their founders were swept up in a vital movement to reclaim the authority of Scripture. The reformers' enthusiasm about the Bible naturally led to a focus on the verbal expression of the *logos*, the printed page of Scripture and its proclamation from the pulpit. The Bible needed to be lifted up and celebrated because it had been lost in the medieval church. But as we approach the 500th anniversary of the Protestant Reformation (1517–2017), it is time to examine how our worship has erred in the opposite direction, becoming too verbose, focusing on speech to the near exclusion of the other wondrous ways in which God's Word comes to us.

Worship that relies too heavily on language drains away the power of words by failing to relate them to the materiality of the world God created. Revitalizing our worship language requires attention to what happens in those spaces when we are not speaking or listening. Think of a conversation with a friend. There are pauses, looks, gestures, touches, and maybe a pot of shared coffee, all of which are an integral part of the conversation. "I'll be thinking of you" becomes an experienced reality as your friend's hand reaches across the table for yours. The relationship between one another is expressed through eye, body, vocal tone, and, of course, words.

Nothing that we have said is meant to diminish the importance of language in worship. We have attended services in which everything looks right, everything goes smoothly, but we never get involved in the conversation with God. Sometimes the language is too high, the words are archaic, the language serves to impress rather than communicate, the prayers are convoluted, not at all the direct expression of a soul in the presence of God. Other times the language is too low, too filled with newest jargon so that there is no sense of tradition or wonder.

What is the language of your service like? Does it encourage the entire crowd to step into the story of the Good News? Do not forget who is listening: the skeptic in the floppy hat, the self-made individual—"I said that I'd do all that I've done"— the shy seeker waiting to call out, "Lord," and the fervent disciple eager to know more and more the new possibilities that God sees for the world. They have all come to this meal, and the Host is eager that everyone of them gets to join in the conversation. Does your language help them to speak plainly what is on their hearts and to hear clearly what is on God's?

Heightened Awareness: A Prelude for Treasures Old and New

> Before I built a wall I'd ask to know
> What I was walling in or walling out,
> And to whom I was like to give offense.[11]

And before we build a new service, we would ask to know what we are walling in or walling out and to whom we were likely to give offense. Until we sit where others sit, stand where others stand, see as others see, and hear as others hear we are not ready to begin reforming a congregation's worship. A heightened awareness of what is happening for the entire community keeps us from reducing the church's reform to our private agenda. That awareness reveals not only what must be preserved but also what the new possibilities are, where in our worship people are yearning and hoping for something more.

Yet heightened awareness alone is not enough. A congregation needs informed, imaginative leadership. Willy Malacher, a consultant to churches reforming their worship, describes the proper balance between the leadership and the congregation:

> Democratic process is not the final answer in worship growth. The process toward discernment of need by consensus seems a better way to arrive at decisions. If an authority person takes the responsibility of decision-making through expertise in a given area, that person must also lead the community to shared ownership of their decision. The ultimate goal is not beautiful new environments, but a people of God pointed toward a new spirit of holiness, a life more intense with the mysterious presence of Christ in their midst.[12]

We reach toward the ultimate goal by training ourselves for

the kingdom, by bringing out of the church's treasure what is old and what is new. Having expanded our appreciation for what the entire congregation experiences in worship, we now listen to the generations before us, the cloud of witnesses who uttered "dark sayings from of old," things that they heard and knew, "the glorious deeds of the Lord." Then, steadied by ancient belief, we examine what is new, those openings in the imagination where the Spirit blows in unexpected ways to re-vitalize our prayers and praise.

Listen to the Cloud

Step from Digital Time into God's Time

Even on the sunniest Sunday of the year a cloud hovers about your congregation. It is not a dark and threatening cloud, but a cloud of light and music. It is the great cloud of witnesses (Hebrews 12), the generations of the past, who in their own fumbling way were faithful to God: the Israelites, the crowds who followed Jesus, the congregations that Paul scolded and loved, the martyrs who died for faith, the nameless believers who witnessed in a million silent ways known only to God, the musicians with ears tuned to heaven and eyes squinted blind at the musical staff, the theologians who spilled ink and blood for their vision of the truth.

In our private lives we are usually oblivious to the cloud. Most of us no longer wake to a ritual of morning prayer as generations of believers did in the past. The very way they marked time kept alive a daily awareness of the cloud of witnesses who had preceded them. How different is our waking and arising every day!

Click.

Sound.

Music.

I turn over and look at the face of my digital clock radio.

6:58

The numbers, solitary and sovereign, stare back at me.

On the old clocks every minute was related to all the others. Time was recorded on a circle, continuous and cohesive. Six fifty-eight was also fifty-eight minutes after six and two minutes before seven. I saw how far I was from the past and how close I was to the future. Now I exist in an encapsulated moment. My waking is not connected to my dreaming. The numbers that marked the visions of the night have flipped from sight. I live in digital time along with the other individuals who come to worship in our churches. We are no longer like our ancestors who day by day lived in the rivers of tradition that flowed from generation to generation.

6:59

I walk over to the television and turn it on. The logo of the local station expands across the screen: a blue-green earth above the curved horizon of the moon. We do not see the world the way the cloud of witnesses did when their feet pounded the earth. Our sense of space, like our sense of time, is utterly different from the cloud's.

7:00

TODAY

The word in bold print appears on my screen. Like the numbers on my digital clock, the word suggests nothing of time past or of time to come.

A destroyed building flashes on the television screen. Ambulances arrive. Medics bring out people on stretchers, some writhing in pain, some dead. The camera pans the faces of families and neighbors. "O my God, my God!" The words slip silently from my lips, not a curse but a prayer, a desperate prayer for the desperate people I see before me. Through that prayer I step into a world which every witness in the cloud has known: the world of the pleading soul, the world of a broken and bleeding humanity, as contemporary as TODAY and as ancient as the cry of a Sumerian supplicant:

May the fury of my lord's heart be quieted toward me.
May the god who is not known be quieted toward me;
May the goddess who is not known be quieted toward me.
. . . .

Although I am constantly looking for help,
  no one takes me by the hand;
When I weep they do not come to my side.
. . . .

O my lord, do not cast thy servant down;
He is plunged into the waters of a swamp;
  take him by the hand.[1]

Drowning and needing a hand—those are the people on the screen before me. And so are the skeptic in the floppy hat and the self-made individual discovering life is beyond their control and the shy disciple retiring into the shadows and the devout follower struggling to be faithful, and so are you, I, the entire congregation, and the psalmist who calls in similar language:

> Save me, O God,
> for the waters have come up to my neck.
> I sink in deep mire,
>   where there is no foothold;
> I have come into deep waters,
>   and the flood sweeps over me
>   (Psalm 69:1-2).

Yet there is this difference between the psalmist and the Sumerian: the psalmist knows by name the Deity to whom he makes his plea. There is no thrashing around for the "god whom I know or do not know," for the "goddess whom I know or do not know." The psalmist aims his cry to a precise, personal center of reality:

> But as for me, my prayer is to you, O LORD.
> At an acceptable time, O God,
>   in the abundance of your steadfast love, answer me.
>   (Psalm 69:13a)

Remembering these words—collected by the worshiping community of Israel, passed on by generations of believers, and read in the church where I grew up—I realize how profoundly we need to listen to the cloud of witnesses. They rescue us from isolating ourselves in digital time. They assure us that we are not at the mercy of some unknown god or goddess, some mercurial force that remains forever hidden from us. The cloud declares to us that behind the dim unknown stands One who has been made known through Jesus Christ. The cloud commands: Step from digital time into God's time.

Oh, listen to the cloud. Listen and be linked to all the faithful witnesses of the past through story, song, and symbol. Listen to the choirs of ancient believers whose voices rumble and thunder through the sounds of your worship. Listen to the cloud in the prelude. The organist sets the molecules of air dancing in the congregation's ears, and you hear the psalmist commanding the worshipers in the Jerusalem temple:

> Praise [God] with trumpet sound;
>   praise him with lute and harp!
> Praise him with tambourine and dance;
>   praise him with strings and pipe!
>   (Psalm 150:3-4)

Listen to the cloud in the congregation's opening hymn. The song expands out of their lungs and mouths and presses against the walls of the church like the praise which fills the vault of heaven:

> "You are worthy, our Lord and God,
> to receive glory and honor and power,
> for you created all things,
> and by your will they existed and were created."
>   (Revelation 4:11)

Listen to the cloud in the reading of the Scriptures. Read from the Old Testament sagas; Abraham and Sarah, Isaac and Rebekah, Jacob and Rachael will be gathered about you. Read from the Prophets, and you will hear their raw and ragged voices demanding from you what they demand from Israel: justice, mercy, righteousness. Read the Gospels, and those who are healed, fed, and taught by Christ will offer their witness to you.

Listen to the cloud in the tradition which Paul has received and which he passes onto Corinth and which is now passed onto your church, "that the Lord Jesus on the night when he was betrayed broke bread. . . . 'Do this in remembrance of me.' "

Listen to the Cloud
Flexible, Real, Alive People Are Speaking

Listening to the cloud is not the same as digging into the past. Although both expressions invite us to explore the history of Christian worship, listening to the cloud is a more ebullient approach than digging. Too often we return to the past hunting for fossils, for some fixed patterns of worship we can copy today, and so we fail to hear our ancestors humming with life. We are like Father Hamster, a priest who taught the Nobel Prize-winning poet Czeslaw Milosz. Father Hamster could

> have shown us that Judaism, contrary to its rival beliefs in antiquity, with their cyclical vision of the world, conceived of Creation in a dynamic way, as a dialogue, a perpetual upsurging of constantly modified questions and constantly modified answers, and that Christianity has inherited this trait . . . . he would have accustomed us to history. But the priest lacked imagination, and he warded off the impingements of the modern world with the shield of a rigid outlook.[2]

Listening to the cloud, we discover that the history of worship is part of that "perpetual upsurging of constantly modified questions and constantly modified answers" which continues in our own time in our own congregations. That "perpetual upsurging" is nothing less than the Spirit working upon us through our life together as a church. We "are being transformed into [the Lord's] image from one degree of glory to another," says Paul (2 Corinthians 3:18), and John confirms his vision: "What we will be has not yet been revealed" (1 John 3:2). Reforming our worship is a way of participating in God's transforming process. It is an act of faithfulness to God who keeps stirring and prodding us to be more completely the people we are meant to be.

Listening to the cloud, we leave behind Father Hamster's "rigid outlook" and we approach the past with a sense for how the juice of life flowed in our ancestors' veins:

To think that the sun rose in the east—that men and women
  were flexible, real, alive—that everything was alive,
To think that you and I did not see, feel, think, nor bear our part,
To think that we are now here and bear our part.[3]

Your church's attitude about history is as important as the
facts of what happened. If people are like Father Hamster, ward-
ing off "the impingements of the modern mind with the shield
of a rigid outlook," the study of the past may be constricting
rather than liberating for your worship. Our goal in this chapter
is not to write a history of Christian worship[4] but to help you
draw on the past as a living resource for the renewal of your
worship.

A question from the cloud: How does your congregation approach the past—looking for fossils or listening for the witness
of flexible, real, alive people?

Listen to the Cloud
Worship Reform Is as Ancient as the Scriptures

Listen to the cloud; yours is not the first congregation to
struggle with renewing its worship. Worship reform reaches
back into the Old Testament:

> Then the king directed that all the elders of Judah and Jerusalem
> should be gathered to him. The king went up to the house of the
> LORD, and with him went all the people of Judah, all the inhab-
> itants of Jerusalem, the priests, the prophets, and all the people,
> both small and great; he read in their hearing all the words of the
> book of the covenant that had been found in the house of the
> LORD. The king stood by the pillar and made a covenant before
> the LORD, to follow the LORD, keeping his commandments, his
> decrees, and his statutes, with all his heart and all his soul, to
> perform the words of this covenant that were written in this book.
> All the people joined in the covenant.
>
> The king commanded the high priest Hilkiah, the priests of the
> second order, and the guardians of the threshold, to bring out of
> the temple of the LORD all the vessels made for Baal, for Asherah,
> and for all the host of heaven; he burned them outside Jerusalem
> in the fields of the Kidron, and carried their ashes to Bethel (2
> Kings 23:1–4).

It was housecleaning time in the Jerusalem temple! The book of the covenant which King Josiah read was probably an early version of Deuteronomy. It "was apparently found in a collection box (12:9) or in some rubbish about to be removed from the temple."[5] God's Word was buried, and it took the leadership of King Josiah and the high priest, Hilkiah, to order that the real rubbish, the idols, be cleared away so that Israel's covenant with the Lord might once more be the basis of the nation's life. Periodically throughout the history of worship, it is housecleaning time again, time to remove whatever has accumulated that obscures the community's relationship to God.

I recall a private housecleaning that for me has become a parable of the church's need to reform its worship again and again. My wife and I were moving from an apartment in which we had lived for several years. In the cellar was a storage closet four feet by four feet and about seven feet high. Like most apartment dwellers we had stuffed that closet full over the years. When we moved, we had to start at the top of the stack which nearly touched the ceiling. We threw out two bald tires, ski wax that had melted and run down over dated checks, dog-eared paperbacks, and a broken car rack. Finally, we came to an old family chest which we opened. On top was some rotting canvas and on the bottom several love letters that we had sent one another when we were courting more than twelve years earlier. We sat down, read them, and relived once more that first thrill of love which had brought us together and led us to make a covenant of faithfulness.

Whenever God's love letters get buried, it is housecleaning time for the worshiping community. Although we have cited 2 Kings 23 because that was "the most significant of all the purifications of the cult,"[6] First and Second Kings record many others: 1 Kings 15:9 ff.; 2 Kings 11:13 ff.; 2 Kings 18:3 ff. In part these accounts reflect the theological bias of the writer who judged every king's reign according to the idealized standard of David. But they also provide an ancient witness to the "perpetual upsurging" of worship renewal.

Such reform does not always involve throwing things out, as if the only way to purify our praise is to claim what already lies within the temple. The biblical process is subtler than that. It includes adapting and modifying the riches offered by popular culture. "Two different worlds met on mount Zion: Israel's central sanctuary and the Canaanite cult of the holy city of Jerusalem. The Canaanite-Jebusite traditions were firmly rooted in this holy place. . . . These alien elements had to be taken up into the worship of Israel, transformed and incorporated into the service of Yahweh."[7]

"Two different worlds met on mount Zion," and they have been meeting ever since that time in the worshiping congregations of God's people. Two different worlds met in the Corinthian church, the new world of the gospel and the old world of pagan loyalties; and the apostle Paul could not ignore that meeting. He had to work out a solution that maintained the integrity of the gospel while respecting the tender sensibilities of Christians whose faith was in an early stage of development (1 Corinthians 8). Two different worlds met in the fourth century church when Constantine accepted Christianity, the secret world of the Christian minority and the dominant culture of the Roman Empire. Two different worlds met in the eighth century reforms of Charlemagne and Alcuin, the simpler worship of Rome and the more ornamental worship of Gaul. Two different worlds met in the uproar of the sixteenth century, the world of the late medieval church and the world of the biblically inspired reformers. Two different worlds met in the black churches of America, the world of African religion and the world of biblical faith.

And two different worlds continue to meet in our churches, the world of the tradition by which we regularly praise God and the world of contemporary life. The question from the cloud of witnesses is not: How will we separate the two worlds? They will not be separated in the present anymore than they were in the past. The question is: Does our worship hold these worlds together in a way that is both faithful to God and expressive of who we are as a community? The congregation of Jerusalem faced this same issue: "When the Ark was installed on mount Zion, the cultic traditions [of the surrounding environment] even penetrated the Israelite sanctuary, but were applied to Yahweh and refashioned in the light of the faith of the Old Testament. The mythical splendour which radiated from the

Syrian-Canaanite traditions served to glorify the place where the God of Israel was present."[8] There was a relationship between the two worlds, between worship and culture, which enriched the congregation's life. But sometimes the two worlds were unevenly joined. The popular myths replaced faith in the Lord instead of enhancing faith. Then once again it was housecleaning time in Jerusalem.

Josiah's temple reform suggests four questions we need to consider for the reform of worship that apply across the ages to our own time:

1. *What do we throw out?* If a practice obscures rather than reveals God's relationship to the world, if it clutters the vision of faith, it is not appropriate to our community. Josiah ditched the idols.

2. *What do we keep?* Much of what we do is deeply expressive of our faith and life; otherwise it would not be bringing us together week after week. We need to hold onto what is good and true and faithful in our worship. Josiah kept the temple.[9]

3. *What do we need to recover?* A close examination of our tradition will reveal that we have lost rich resources which can restore a sharper sense of our historical identity. Josiah once again celebrated the Passover which had been ignored for years.

4. *What do we need to adapt from popular culture?* There may be forms of expression in society that can be adapted and used to make our worship connect with our daily lives. When Josiah renewed the covenant, he drew on a form of treaty common to the ancient Near East, though modified by Israel's faith.[10]

Housecleaning time in the church involves carefully weighing all four of these questions. No congregation can use everything from the vast treasure of tradition. Even the apostles had to be selective when they shared the good news about Jesus. Peter, for example, "adapted his teachings to the needs of the moment and did not make an ordered exposition of the sayings of the Lord."[11] In a similar fashion Paul tailored his message to the state of the congregation: "And so, brothers and sisters, I could not speak to you as spiritual people, but rather as people of the flesh, as infants in Christ. I fed you with milk, not solid food, for you were not ready for solid food. Even now you are still not ready, for you are still of the flesh" (1 Corinthians 3:1–3a). If Peter and Paul were flexible enough to adapt their presentation of the gospel to meet the needs of their congregations, we can do the same. As long as we listen to the cloud of witnesses and keep God's love letters, the Scriptures, before us, we are free to modify worship to meet the needs of our time.

A question from the cloud: What kind of housecleaning does your worship need? What needs to be thrown out? Kept? Recovered? Adapted?

Listen to the Cloud
Hidden Glories Are Waiting for You

There is no historical absolute that we can derive from the past to tell us, "This is the way the congregation must always worship." Not even the Bible—central as it is to church reform—provides a permanent, ideal pattern of worship. We have already seen that the Scriptures reveal a dynamic community of faith that was periodically renewing its life of prayer and praise.

Furthermore, it is impossible for us to arrive at a pure interpretation of the Bible which is unmuddied by the limits of our own position in history. We tend to be arrogant about our understanding, thinking that we have come closer to the truth than any other generation: "the interpretive inadequacy of our predecessors is assumed by all of us, however we explain it." [12] We rarely acknowledge the complexities of our interpretations but instead "are more likely to ask, am I right or wrong? And we like to be more right than anyone before us, including the author if necessary." [13] Yet the end of time will reveal the perceptions of this age to be no less conditioned by our historical situation than those who went before us. That is why we need to listen to many regions of the cloud and not only one or two. Each corrects the other, and all together they give a fuller vision of truth.

The more regions of the cloud we listen to, the more we will understand that no church's worship has been pure and perfect. Like the action of any "flexible, real, alive" people, worship has drawn the best and the worst from the human heart. For there is a horrible as well as an inspiring side to the history of worship.

God's people imprisoned, tortured, and executed one another over the form and meaning of the church's praise.

D. M. Thomas's novel *The White Hotel* concludes with a scene in which the central characters, estranged during their lives, meet in a transfigured state beyond time, space, and the brutalities of history.[14] If a novelist can hold up such a vision, is it too much to hope that the reformation of our worship might reflect the heavenly reconciliation of those Christians who once fought each other to the death?

If we go back into the past with Father Hamster's "rigid outlook," we may confirm our own rigidities, our own prejudices against the way other folks worship. We will find heroes in our tradition and villains in the others. But if we think of all the worshipers who have gone before us as a cloud of witnesses, now eternally joined together in the praise of God despite their earthly battles, then we can claim the truth which each left behind without holding on to the divisions of the past. This does not mean reducing worship to an ecumenical pudding. Rather we celebrate what is good and true in each tradition while drawing on the wisdom of others to correct and strengthen us where we are weak. Listening to the cloud we realize that there are twelve gates—not one!—into the city of God, that there are many rooms—not one!—in the place which Christ has prepared for us. Gates that were closed and rooms that were locked to our ancestors are now open to us.

Hidden glories are waiting for us in the cloud. Tradition sometimes preserves biblical meanings and insights that our particular church misses because it views the Scriptures through a preconception of right or wrong interpretation. In few aspects of Christian worship is this more apparent than in the celebration of the Lord's Supper. The church in which I grew up kept the Lord's Supper primarily as a commemoration of Christ's death. That was apparent not only in the words that we used but also in the grim faces of those who served the bread and wine and the invariably sad organ music that accompanied the meal. A funereal solemnity pervades all of my early memories at Christ's table, and I have since discovered my experience to be characteristic of that of a great many worshipers. Certainly the recalling of Christ's death is one important meaning of the meal. But only one! "The Lord's Supper was, from the first, a multifaceted, multidimensional experience of Christian worship."[15] Tradition can help us reclaim that "multifaceted, multidimensional experience" which our church may have lost.

In "The First Apology of Justin Martyr," a defense of Christianity from around 155, we discover that the Lord's Supper recalled for the early church not only Christ's death, but also his entire incarnation. Breaking bread and passing the cup, they recalled, "Jesus Christ our Saviour, being incarnate by the Word of God, took flesh and blood for our salvation. . . ."[16] Likewise, "The Apostolic Tradition of Hippolytus," written about fifty years later, interpreted the meal as a celebration of *both* "His death and resurrection,"[17] and when the bread was passed, it was accompanied with the words "The Bread of Heaven in Christ Jesus."[18] These traditions show that the Lord's Supper in the early church expressed more of the totality of Christ, not only Christ the Savior who died for us, but also Christ the Word made flesh, Christ the risen Lord, Christ the bread of eternal life. And that is only the beginning.

The "multifaceted, multidimensional experience" of the Lord's Supper may also have trembled with other meanings and realities: Christ dining with anyone who has opened the door to him (Revelation 3:20), Christ, the sacrificed lamb (1 Corinthians 5:7), Christ sharing the meal in his kingdom at the end of time (Luke 22:30), Christ coming again (1 Corinthians 11:26). Does your church, like the early church, express the totality of who Christ was and is through the Lord's Supper?

If a preacher's sermons proclaim only a single aspect of Christ, the congregation soon grumbles that it is not receiving the full gospel. Yet many of us celebrate a truncated gospel in the way we keep the Lord's Supper. We listen only to the region of the cloud with which we are familiar and diminish our worship by ignoring the richness of Christ's reality at the table. If this is the case with your church, renew your worship by listening to more of the cloud. Develop a series of services to explore what a "multifaceted, multidimensional experience" the Lord's Supper was in the early church. The list of various scriptural meanings which we have cited in the last two pages can provide an initial outline:

Christ who died for us.
Christ, the risen Lord.
Christ, the bread of life.
Christ knocking at the door.
Christ, the lamb.
Christ sharing his feast in the kingdom.

Do not think only of sermons. Talk in your worship committee about music and prayers that might reflect more accurately the dimension of Christ's reality you are trying to catch sight of again. Not everything should be in a minor key or a meditative mood. Christ sharing his feast in the kingdom is a matter for glad and joyful song.

Do not spring these ideas unannounced on the congregation, but prepare people gradually over time. Always keep clear the goal: to know Christ more fully at his table, even as the early church did.

If your worship committee leads the congregation sensitively through this kind of program, the church's pastoral care will be strengthened. The skeptic in the floppy hat may finally hear Christ knocking at the heart's door and open it. The self-made individual may feed on the bread of life and find release from the illusion that we control existence. The reticent disciple may step out of the shadows to face the risen Lord. The faithful disciple may be helped in a struggle of Christian principle by a vision of the kingdom to come as the bread and wine are served.

To claim the hidden glories that are waiting for us in the cloud is "to know more of the fullness of God." It is to discover what I once discovered when I was enveloped by fog on the top of a mountain. Because earlier it had been a clear day, I assumed that I was in a passing cloud and that all the other peaks were still standing in sunny blue sky. But when I descended and looked up, I saw the top of every mountain was connected to the same cloud through which I had climbed. Our churches share one vast cloud of witnesses, but each tends to know its immediate surroundings with only a vague awareness of the rest. As good and meaningful as our own tradition may be, we often miss the opportunity to grow in the Spirit that comes from climbing into new regions of the cloud. For example, when I was a child, I learned church music within a denomination whose musical tradition had been clearly defined at the time of Martin Luther, and largely by the reformer himself. The 578 hymns in our denominational hymnal included many texts and tunes[19] which had been born, developed, and given perpetual care by Lutherans since Reformation times.

We valued the strength and longevity of our tradition. It helped us remember clearly who we are and what standards we are responsible to uphold.

It was comforting to us to note the large proportion of German Lutheran compositions our hymnal contained. In fact, the editors had designed the book to assist us in identifying them; the denominational affiliation of the authors of all hymns was noted in the index, as was the original language of translated hymns. Anyone could simply turn over a few pages to learn something of an author's theological posture and the country of origin of any hymn in the book.

This seemed important to us, for we knew that those chorales, which for so long had been identified as "Lutheran," had emerged from our ancestors' struggle in the Protestant Reformation. This sixteenth-century housecleaning had been a time of renewal and restoration of health to the people's worship. Our hymnal was a living record of our denomination's Golden Age.

Our Sunday school hymnal was not a denominational publication, however, and in the course of exploring it, we discovered that some of the tunes were noticeably different from the rest. Once introduced to us, and before anyone could direct otherwise, these songs had become our favorites.

"Can we sing 'I Am Thine, O Lord' again next Sunday?" people would ask. And we often did sing that song, for all present were filled with joy at the sound of such exuberant singing.

There was something delightful about this music. We were drawn naturally to it. It was easy to learn because the last several lines following each stanza were always the same. This "refrain" was so simple that most people memorized it the first time we sang it through.

Many years later, study of the theory of music would help me to understand the different kind of musical satisfaction we had felt in singing those Sunday school songs. The ancient chorales we sang in church often sounded a different chord under each melody note.[20] In the "Passion Chorale," for example, at least one and sometimes two chordal sounds are on nearly every syllable of the text.

This can be exciting to those singing. It expresses strength and vigor. The many changes of melody notes along with the chord changes can function to draw our attention to the text, for we are required to be alert if we do not want to be left behind in the singing.

Excitement, strength, vigor, attentiveness, pride of tradition—these are all important qualities of good hymn singing. Human beings feel satisfaction in experiencing them.

But the music of "I Am Thine, O Lord" expresses other qualities. Melody, harmony, and text are organized to sing a unified message: a cry to Jesus, Beloved Friend, whose sacrifice on the cross was for each one personally as well as for the whole world. There is a vision of heavenly peace and desire for earthly strength and hope. As in "O Sacred Head" the cross is central to the faithful one's address to the Savior, but the music by W. H. Doane makes it seem an instrument of triumph rather than torture.

The tune which carries "I Am Thine, O Lord" communicated

O sa-cred head, sore wound-ed, De- filed and put to scorn.

to our youthful souls qualities such as comfort and secure acceptance. Because it is so easily singable, we felt encouraged to join in. The chords change relatively seldom—usually once each measure—so we are confident that the harmony will hold still while we seek some consonant tone to join in singing.

Only three chords are used in all four measures of this example. There are double that number in the "Passion Chorale" example. When hearing the same sounds repeated, we have a reassuring sense of returning to familiar territory.

We sang that hymn with all the exuberance of youth savoring forbidden fruit because we began to sense among the older people a certain disapproval of our musical choices. They reminded us that this was not "our tradition" and implied that that fact alone should be understood as reason for discontinuing use of this music. It did not come from their region of the cloud.

"How stupid!" we thought. "How old-fashioned!" we said. How unfair it seemed to have our choices of music controlled by practices of nameless, faceless people in some long ago time.

Here the storytelling ends, but in fact there is no end to the

story. It continues everywhere human beings gather to worship. What shall we do? On what basis shall we include certain hymns and prayers and exclude others? Is our denomination's tradition the only criterion to be considered? Not long ago the answer to that question might have been a firm "Yes!"

"If it was good enough for our ancestors, it is good enough for me."

"We've always sung that hymn."

"We've never sung that hymn."

And on. And on.

Is there an ear which has never heard these words spoken with full dramatic conviction? They are often the immediate and unpremeditated response to the introduction of something unfamiliar into worship.

But a classic question requires a fresh response from every age. Each congregation must confront anew the challenge of balancing seemingly opposing energies. Any who would lead people in authentic worship of God must define their responsibilities to include continuing examination of both the people's history and their hopes.

We draw strength and inspiration from the past. The cloud of witnesses gives comfort and reassurance to us, for they too were striving to live out the faith they held. Their specific words and their songs are particularly precious to us because they sang and prayed them. Still, traditions must be seen through eyes fully open and focusing clearly. A tinted lens or a muddy perspective could prevent us from understanding the full picture. History and tradition have been recorded for us in vast libraries. We need not wonder or discuss without benefit of record. The public, seminary, or church library will offer light for our endless examination of the cloud.

As a youthful Sunday school pianist, I had no perspective from which to judge the theological or musical worthiness of "I Am Thine, O Lord." I had no idea that information on hymnody was available through books. My knowledge of church music was bounded on all sides by the two hymnals used regularly in our church building and the musical practices of the musicians who had served our congregation during my lifetime.

Who would have dreamed that in the world there were hundreds, even thousands of gospel and camp meeting songs similar to the few, like "I Am Thine, O Lord," in which our Sunday school took such delight? These songs, written and promoted in America from about 1800, were intended to draw exactly that response from listeners. Louis Benson writes, "Of the tunes to which the Camp Meeting Hymns were sung the leaders demanded nothing more than contagiousness and effectiveness."[21]

Books and magazine articles can help us answer many questions which arise as we plan worship. John Spencer Curwen interviewed the famous singer of gospel songs, Ira Sankey, in 1885 and wrote:

> There has been plenty of debate over these American gospel song-tunes. Are they legitimate church music, and if not, is it wise to employ a musical idiom in the prayer-meeting and mission service which cannot be tolerated in the church? . . .
>
> Yet, after the musician has vented his spleen upon this degenerate psalmody, an important fact remains. Music in worship is a means, not an end, and we are bound to consider how far these tunes serve their end in mission work, which after all, has not musical training for its object, so much as the kindling of the divine spark in the hearts of the worshippers. Without doubt these songs touch the common throng; they match the words to which they are sung, and carry them.[22]

Mr. Curwen's words transport us through time to the age in which gospel and camp-meeting songs were freshly born. Yet he asks the same questions which are heard today.

"Are these tunes really usable in church?" (Do they fit our concept of traditional music?)

"If they are not appropriate for church use, should Christians be singing them anywhere?" (In Sunday school, for instance?)

"From what source comes the power of these tunes to kindle the 'divine spark in the hearts of the worshippers'?" (Aren't they too emotional?)

Without supplying direct answers, Mr. Curwen has helped us by proposing the questions. Perhaps he might have approved "I Am Thine, O Lord" for our Sunday school. After all, music which engages the singers and listeners with uncomplicated expressions of faith seems an appropriate choice for youthful Christians. Yet in our Sunday school story the objections to their use did not center on appropriateness. Criticism was directed at their not reflecting "our tradition."

Listening to the cloud, we discover that decisions about community worship should be based on more than one question. The theology and the literary and musical quality of the hymn must be examined as well as its appropriateness for the community, the worship space, and the time. "Our tradition or not our tradition" is but one matter to be examined. We must look carefully at other questions as well. We no more want to constrict the gospel by a narrow understanding of what is musically right and wrong than by a narrow understanding of the Lord's Supper. In these ecumenical, multiracial, transcontinental times, what is "our tradition"? Happily, the definitions are, like the cloud, rounding off at the edges.

Looking back to the genesis of any of our denominations may be quite helpful. It is possible to learn from books what was done, sung, and said. But it is not enough to observe only the circumstantial evidence. More important by far is seeking some understanding of the spirit of the events. Remember: we are dealing with "flexible, real, alive" people.

We know that Martin Luther listened to his sixteenth-century cloud and valued all the good that had gone before. He claimed plainchant for its serene beauty as a symbol of God's eternal presence. The melodies already had deep significance for him and were familiar to the people. Luther also drew on his experience of exquisite polyphony by master composers to suggest shapes of melodies he would adapt for some of the chorales.[23] In the music which he wrote Luther "neither disdained the use of older traditional materials nor shrank from revolutionary changes in the interest of German speech rhythm and popular appeal. For he wanted hymns and chants to be sung by the congregation as well as by the choir."[24] That intention bears a striking resemblance to that which motivated composers of many gospel and camp-meeting songs. Using musical materials of their own times, each sought to draw people closer to God.

God's continuing revelation is the center of our concern for worship renewal. Church music is most faithful when it expresses the true spirit of those living people gathered to worship God.

Many voices in the cloud have known in their age what your people are living today. They have sung it out and written it down, and you can hear them if you listen to the cloud. Both chorales and gospel songs are sounding in the cloud. Your congregation may wish to use both or neither of them. Gospel songs are powered by repetition and emotional content. Chorales operate in a lower gear, passing poetry of a sturdy faith through our minds and hearts at a more moderate tempo. Perhaps other music in the cloud matches your own collective song more closely.

Our corporate prayers and songs will always reflect the particular tradition to which we belong. And that is good and right. It provides a secure foundation, a clear identity, and continuing encouragement in the faith. But we must be careful not to tune out voices that come from other regions of the cloud because they do not sing as we do. Listening to the cloud, we can avoid grating pronouncements of arrogance and perceived superiority, all of which are a modern version of those condemnations that led to religious wars in the sadder moments of the past.

Instead, let the ringing voices of the radiantly faithful hold our attention. To realize that human beings in another church or in another part of the world have shared our convictions and our warmed hearts can only increase our joy. Openness in worship allows us to listen and benefit from every region of the cloud so ". . . that we may ever hereafter serve and please thee in newness of life, to the honor and glory of thy Name. . . ."[25]

A question from the cloud: Is your church open to searching for the hidden glories that might deepen and enrich its worship?

Listen to the Cloud
Structure and Spontaneity, Clergy and Congregation— the Balance Keeps Slipping

Little more than fifteen years after the death and resurrection of Christ the church was already facing a major question about its worship: how do we balance spontaneity and structure? The balance was slipping in the church at Corinth. Spontaneity was threatening to overwhelm structure and bring chaos to the community's worship. The word "community" is crucial. In 1 Corinthians 12–14 Paul insists that worship is a corporate action of the entire community. He scolds the Corinthians for using their gifts divisively, but he assumes everyone will continue to contribute to the church's worship, each bringing "a hymn, a lesson, a revelation, a tongue, or an interpretation" (1 Corinthians 14:26). Paul lays down principles rather than a set pattern for the Corinthians:

"Pursue love and strive for the spiritual gifts, especially that you may prophesy" (1 Corinthians 14:1).

"I will pray with the spirit, but I will pray with the mind also; I will sing praise with the spirit, but I will sing praise with the mind also" (1 Corinthians 14:15b,c).

"But all things should be done decently and in order" (1 Corinthians 14:40).

Paul is trying to keep the balance between structure and spontaneity to ensure the health of the entire community. He insists that whatever happens should "edify" the whole congregation and not just the individual who is offering a gift. Paul beats on the theme like a drum, using the word "edify" five times in chapter 14.

> Paul was able to bring freedom of the Spirit and the restrictions of liturgy together in the self-same service because he saw everything in the light of the one aim: the οἰκοδομή (building up of the Church). For this reason, he is able to allow speaking with tongues, under certain conditions, and at the same time to repeat liturgical formulae, without giving rise to anarchy with the one or lifelessness with the other. It is precisely in this *harmonious combination of freedom and restriction* that there lies the greatness and uniqueness of the early Christian service of worship.[26]

By building up the community, worship is to embody that divine love which Paul has rhapsodized as the greatest of all gifts in 1 Corinthians 13. We tend to isolate this famous passage from its context and shrink love down to the size of our individual relationship with God. But chapters 12 and 14 as well as the ceremonial imagery—"a noisy gong or a clanging cymbal"—

make clear that Paul's hymn to love belongs to the worshiping community.

Does it belong to yours?

Unless worship helps the entire community to offer up their gifts to God, it is a poor expression of that love which is "not envious or boastful or arrogant or rude" (1 Corinthians 13:4-5). If the skeptic in the floppy hat gets the impression that worship is nothing more than listening to the preacher or the choir, he will either stand on the periphery for the rest of his life or walk away. But if he senses a community which shares God's love through its prayers and praise, he may feel the Spirit prompting him to give away his doubt and step into the circle.

In the beginning, Christian worship was not a performance by the few for the many. In the upper room, on the night on which he was betrayed, Jesus and his companions ate together and sang what were in all probability psalms (Matthew 26:30). This was their practice already, coming from the tradition of their ancestors, their cloud of witnesses. Descriptions of singing, dancing, and playing musical instruments are abundant in the Old Testament. And, of course, the Jews counted the Psalms as their own song.

From Matthew's brief account it appears that the music of the Christian church in its prenatal stage was essentially tradition adapted to the needs of the worshipers at the moment. Matthew mentions no hymnals and no instruments to accompany their singing at the Last Supper. The company must have known the music by heart. They probably sang without leadership, finding comfort as they remembered all the many times these psalms had been sung at traditional meals in the past. They recalled the God who had brought their people out of Egypt centuries before and who, they believed, would bring them through the increasing heat of their current situation. It was probably the best sort of singing by a community that we could envision. Everybody knows the words and music; nobody is glued to a book or straining to lean toward the light; and some people may close their eyes as their song becomes prayer.

Things obviously had begun very well. Music and prayer belonged to the entire congregation, and that was the pattern which continued after the death and resurrection of Christ. Church members taught and guided one another's development by means of "psalms, hymns, and spiritual songs" (Colossians 3:16). We do not have written record of the tunes they sang, for music notation was not devised until many centuries later, but the Bible has brought to us many texts thought to have been sung in the first few centuries of the church's life. For example, The Magnificat, "My soul magnifies the Lord . . .'" (Luke 1:46-55), The Benedictus, "Blessed be the Lord God of Israel . . .'" (Luke 1:68–79), and The Nunc Dimittus, "'Master, now you are dismissing your servant in peace . . .'" (Luke 2:29–32) all may be songs from a community of Jewish Christians called the *Anawim*, "the Poor Ones."[27] In adapting these songs to his account of Jesus' life, Luke left a permanent reminder of how the gospel echoed through the music of the church.

For the next three centuries the entire congregation continued to sing, pray, and offer its gifts whenever Christians gathered to worship. Around 155 Justin Martyr described how everyone stood to offer prayers together, and some fifty years later Hippolytus recorded that after the Bishop's exhortation the congregation was given an opportunity to ask questions. Both services reveal a balance between structure and spontaneity, clergy and congregation. The people even brought their own bread and wine to offer at the Lord's table. In fact, the ancient term for worshipers is "offerers"—that is, people who through their gifts at the table offer up all they have and are to God. The change of term from "offerers" to "communicants" which was completed during the medieval period "reflects an immense shift of emphasis in devotion. It goes along with a change in the status of the laity from participants in a corporate act with the celebrant to passive beneficiaries. . . ."[28]

The congregation increasingly began to lose its voice in worship after the Emperor Constantine accepted Christianity and recognized the church along with Licinius through The Edict of Milan in 313. Christian worship went public. It moved from private homes, where Christians had met secretly to avoid persecution, to imperial public buildings called basilicas. Think back to the exercise in chapter 2, taking a different pew in your church. If changing your position in familiar space can alter your experience of worship, imagine what happened when those fourth-century Christians moved their services into the monumental meeting halls of the empire. Some worshipers, glad as they were to be free from the threat of persecution, probably grumbled after the service about the loss of closely knit community that they used to feel when they huddled about a table in the more intimate quarters of a private home and remembered their own cloud of witnesses. The larger space of the basilicas and the greater number of worshipers inevitably led to more responsibility for the clergy. Set apart from the rest of the people by their ornate clothing, the presiding ministers gathered behind the table at one end of the hall and looked out at the congregation facing forward.

Worship expanded in length and increased in formality. "Now more [set] actions, musical parts, and lengthy prayers were added."[29] There was less room for the people's expression of call and response with God. The balance between structure and spontaneity, clergy and congregation was tilting toward fixed order and high clerical control.

Listen to the cloud and imagine being with the fourth-century Christians who gradually became more observers than participants, more communicants than offerers. Perhaps at first they were pleased to have Communion cups of precious metals and splendid processionals of the ministers. "This is what church should be," they might have said. "This befits the worship of God, who surely deserves ceremony equal to that of the emperor's court." But the oldest living members of the church were probably troubled at the differences evident in the beloved Christian community. Civil acceptability and the relaxing of requirements for membership in the church had spurred growth in numbers but not in conviction. How different things seemed from those house church meetings when only professed believers were present! The younger ones must have found it difficult to be patient with the protestations of their elders against the new ways of worshiping. They may have answered, "Why, some of those early Christians couldn't even carry a tune and others would make up melodies as they sang. You never knew what to expect once they started singing! Listen how beautifully the choir's voice echoes in the nave."

"Nave," from a Latin word meaning "ship," was the term for the main body of the great building in which the church now worshiped. The Apostolic Constitution, from around 375, draws vividly on this nautical metaphor: "When thou callest an assembly of the church, as one that is the commander of a great ship, appoint the assemblies to be made with all possible skill; charging the Deacons, as mariners, to prepare places for the brethren, as for passengers, with all due care and decorum."[30]

By the time of the Protestant Reformation the captains of the ship, the clergy, had taken full control of the vessel and the rest of the crew was left with little to do. Although the medieval ideal was that "people should meet together, live together, argue together, work together and set up a whole small township around the site of the future cathedral,"[31] that community vision was not apparent in the worship. The Lord's table, which had once stood as a witness to Christ's presence in the midst of the people, was now against the wall and obscured from the congregation's view by an ornamented screen, the rood screen, which also separated priests from laity.

The architecture of the building reflected the architecture of the worship: services acted, prayed, and sung by the clergy while the congregation looked on. Lay participation had vanished. The congregation's voice was not required, in fact, was restricted from participating in the liturgy. By the Middle Ages, the liturgical music of trained choirs was far too complex for the people to join in singing. Most lay people could not understand or speak the language used. And if they could, they might not have heard what was prayed anyway. The clergy believed that the prayer consecrating the bread was so holy "that the congregation should not even hear it; therefore, the celebrant began to whisper the prayer. The result of all this was that the lay people lost all participation in the regular Sunday service. They had nothing to do; they did not even understand what was going on."[32]

Books were written suggesting ways the congregation could meditate upon the mass while the clergy carried on the worship.

Although the meditations centered on the different parts of the service, they in no way involved the congregation as a corporate body. Each worshiper engaged in an isolated act of devotion. The original vital impulse of the entire community offering its worship to God had faded away.

Gone were the people's gifts.

Gone were the people's prayers.

Gone were the people's responses.

Gone were the people's bread and wine.

Gone were the people's songs.

The balance between spontaneity and structure, clergy and congregation had more than slipped. It had disappeared. However, the people's urge to praise God through music would not be stifled. They sang psalms, hymns, and spiritual songs just as the early Christians had, only now their own music was offered outside the church walls. Those "flexible, real, alive" people had an irrepressible need to sing their faith. Sooner or later the "perpetual upsurging" of the Spirit that prompted their song was bound to erupt inside the church. It did. In 1517 Martin Luther nailed his ninety-five theses to the door of the Wittenberg Cathedral, and we can still hear the echoes from his hammering.

Listen to the cloud during the sixteenth and seventeenth centuries. It is filled with conflicting voices and radically different understandings of the church, the Bible, and worship. Yet here and there, one way or another, the balance between structure and spontaneity, clergy and congregation is at least beginning to reappear. Lutherans are singing chorales. Calvinists are singing psalms with such devotion that they carry their precious psalters under their arms down the streets of Geneva. Follow them to the medieval church of St. Pierre and you will hear the sound of saw and hammer. Look inside and you will see people taking down the rood screen which separated the congregation from the altar and priests. The pulpit is being moved to make it more accessible to the listener. Step aside while they bring in a table and place it among the people for the celebration of the Lord's Supper.[33] It is housecleaning time in this church. It is housecleaning time throughout all the churches. The "perpetual upsurging of constantly modified questions and constantly modified answers" runs through the sixteenth and seventeenth centuries in streams of ink from the pens of theologians and gathers into rivers of belief and practice that refuse to flow into a single pattern of worship.

Yet in bits and pieces—

The people's gifts are returning.

The people's prayers are returning.

The people's responses are returning.

The people's bread and wine are returning.

The people's songs are returning.

None of this happens in one fell swoop, and the reformers are often frustrated in their efforts. Martin Luther wanted to restore the Word of God to the people through biblical preaching, but he ran into "the appalling ignorance of the parochial clergy."[34] John Calvin "in the pursuit of [his] lifelong desire" for weekly Communion was "continually rebuffed by the Genevan Council."[35] And when Thomas Cranmer gathered into a single book the prayers and responses that once were the exclusive property of the clergy in England,[36] he found that the laity "do wilfully and damnably abstain and refuse to come to their parish churches."[37] Worship reform was no easier in the age of reformation than it is nowadays in your own church. If your worship committee wants to commiserate with some people about resistance and rejection, listen to the cloud.

Even when radical worship reform happens, there is a tendency over time to slip back into patterns of clergy-dominated services. We have a striking illustration of this from a workshop with an association of Baptist churches. One of the participants said, "We call ourselves the Free Church, yet I find our worship notably unfree. It seems that the basic pattern in the churches where I have been pastor and the ones I've visited is the same: three hymns, a prayer, and a sermon—nearly everything done by the pastor. Where did our freedom go?" What an honest minister! His comments could be modified to express the distance which many worshipers feel between their current practice and what they sense must have been the impulse that gave their particular tradition its original vitality.

During the workshop we listened to the cloud to discover how the Free Church became the unfree Free Church. We began by returning to the letters and publications of John Smyth, the English Separatist—a term designating those "separating" themselves from the established Church of England—who wanted "to reduce the worship and ministery of the church to the primitive Apostolique institution from which as yet it is so farr distant."[38] Although "there have been, throughout the whole history of Christendom, groups of Christians who have resembled the Baptists,"[39] Smyth founded the first modern Baptist church in 1609. Because he did not believe in the use of printed materials in worship, we have no prayer books from which to gather a description of his services. However, we do have a letter from two worshipers, Hugh and Anne Bromhead, to their cousin William Hamerton, which gives an account of their services:

> We begynne wth a prayer, after reade some one or two chapters of the bible, gyve the sence therof, and cōferr vpon the same, that done wee lay aside oure bookes, and after a solemne prayer made by the .1. speaker he propoundeth some text ov^t of the scripture and prophesieth ov^t of the same by the space of one hower, or the Quarters of an hower. After him standeth vp A .2. speaker and prophesieth ov^t of the same text the like tyme and place sometyme more sometyme lesse. After him the .3. the .4. the .5. &c as the tyme will geve leave. Then the .1. speaker cōcludeth wth prayer as he began wth prayer wth an exhortation to cōtribution to the poore, wch collection being made is also cōcluded wth prayer. This morning exercise begynes at eight of the clock, and cōtinueth vnto twelve of the clocke, the like course and exercise is observed in the afternoone from .2. of the clock vnto .5. or .6. of the clocke. last of all the execution of the govermēt of the church is handled.[40]

Speakers 1, 2, 3, 4, 5, etc.—that is some contrast to "nearly everything done by the minister"! Early Baptist worship, like the worship of the early church, was highly congregational. Smyth makes clear that all worshipers are responsible for speaking the truth they know: "The Spirit is quenched by silence when fit matter is revealed to one that siteth by & he withholdeth it in tyme of prophecying."[41] Smyth was righting the balance between structure and spontaneity.

Yet Smyth had no illusion that he had formulated the ideal worship pattern. His own writing reveals that he was in a state of flux, refining and reforming his insights from year to year. For example, in 1607 he published *Principles and Inferences Concerning the Visible Church.* Then just a year later he modified the contents of that tract with another work bearing one of those charmingly complete titles typical of the period:

THE DIFFERENCES OF THE
Churches of the seperation:
contayning,
A DESCRIPTION OF THE LEITOURGIE AND
Ministerie of the visible Church.
Annexed:
AS A CORRECTION AND SUPPLEMENT TO A LITLE
treatise lately published, bearing title:
Principles and Inferences, concerning the visible Church.

Mark the word "leitourgie," "liturgy," in the title. It is a term usually associated with Roman Catholics, Lutherans, and Anglicans; yet here it is in an early Free Church treatise. Its demise in Free Church circles shows how a tradition loses its roots, disowning language and concepts that are part of its heritage. The term means quite simply "the work of the people" and that is why John Smyth put it on the title page. "Liturgy" says exactly what Smyth understands as central about worship: namely, that it is the work of all God's people and not just the clergy. When Free Church people use the term "liturgy" or "liturgical" they are being more than ecumenical. They are being faithful to their own tradition which tried to restore the balance between structure and spontaneity, clergy and congregation.

Smyth was skittish that readers might hold it against him that he was already changing his mind again about the nature of the church's worship:

> And although in this writing somthing ther is which overtwharteth my former judgmēt in some treatises by mee formerly published: Yet I would intreat the reader not to impute that as a fault vnto mee: rather it should be accounted a vertue to retract erroers: Know therfor that latter though[t]s oft tymes are better then the former: & I do professe this (that no man account it straunge), that

I will every day as my erroers shalbe discovered confesse them & renounce them.[42]

In changing from "former thoughts" to "latter thoughts," Smyth was not averse to listening to other regions of the cloud. While maintaining that he did not approve all the practices of those who differed from him, he was ecumenical enough to write: "wee have (wee willingly & thankfully acknowledge) receaved much light of truth from their writings, for which mercy we alwayes bless our God: & for which help wee alwayes shall honour them in the Lord and in the truth."[43]

What emerges out of reading this early Free Church leader is more than a liturgy that allowed free prayers, that is, prayers offered spontaneously rather than from a prayer book. We sense a freedom to reform the church's worship that draws on Scripture and other traditions while following the leading of the Spirit. "We call ourselves the Free Church, yet I find our worship notably unfree," observed the pastor at the workshop. The unfree Free Church may find new life in reclaiming John Smyth's openness to reformation which is scriptural, Spirit led, and ecumenical without being wishy-washy. That was the Free Church ethos at its best and it continued on after Smyth in other Baptists, including the many who did not follow him in all his beliefs. A Baptist Confession of 1646, drawn up by seven churches, evinces the same combination of bold conviction and openness:

> Also we confess, that we know but in part, and that we are ignorant of many things which we desire and seek to know. And if any shall do us that friendly part, to show us from the Word of God that we see not, we shall have cause to be thankful to God and to them. But if any man shall impose on us anything that we see not to be commanded by our Lord Jesus Christ, we should rather . . . die. . . ."[44]

The pulse of Free Church worship kept beating strongly in the congregations of New England during the colonial period. Doug Adams has documented how

> From the landing of the Mayflower through the American Revolution, the majority of free church clergy probably spent more time interacting with worshipers around the communion table than they did preaching from pulpits. Worship patterns varied by denomi-

nation and region; but frequent communion and substantive lay contributions to the preaching and praying characterized much free church worship in seventeenth and eighteenth century America.[45]

"Where did our freedom go?" asked the baffled pastor at the workshop.

John Skoglund traces its decline to the nineteenth century, to the influence of revivalism and the preacher as performer.[46] The revival meeting was designed to climax in a sermon and an altar call so that the preacher became the central actor in the drama of the service. Revivalism rebuilt the order, style, and even physical setting of the service. The questioning and debate that followed sermons in many colonial churches[47] was eliminated to make room for the altar call. The prayers and offerings were moved to the beginning of the service so that they no longer represented the people's response to the declared Word of God. The action was not among the people but up front where the preacher held forth. And up front was in some cases a new location because the insides of churches were often redesigned to accommodate the revival style. While the congregation once sat on three sides around the Lord's table, they now all faced in the same direction and looked at the minister who was on a raised platform.

Some great things came out of these revival services: people accepted Jesus Christ as Lord and the force of the gospel was felt in the larger society. But once a community was evangelized, it left the congregation with a service that focused on the minister's performance rather than on the people's praise. The preacher monopolized the service just as the medieval clergy monopolized the mass. Once again the balance between structure and spontaneity, clergy and congregation tilted overwhelmingly toward order and control.

The original vital impulse of the entire community offering its worship to God was lost again. The same process we traced as the church moved from homes to basilicas to cathedrals repeated itself in a new way in the history of the Free Church. After the fires of revival subsided, the established Free Church congregations were almost as passive as those of the late Middle Ages.

Gone — again! — were the people's prayers.
Gone — again! — were the people's responses.
Gone — again! — were the people's bread and wine.

But this time, thank God, the songs remained. Perhaps that is why Free Church congregations tend to sing hymns so energetically; it is the major form of participation that is theirs.

Listening to the cloud, we discover a basic truth about our worship life: the balance between structure and spontaneity, clergy and congregation keeps slipping. The burst of Spirit which sets a tradition into motion and which is shared by the entire community settles over time into increasingly rigid forms that are dominated by the leadership. Therefore, churches need periodically to recover the force which first gave them their identity and energy.[48] The apostle Paul knew this. Luke writes that on his third missionary journey, "Paul had decided to sail past Ephesus, so that he might not have to spend time in Asia, he was eager to be in Jerusalem, if possible, on the day of Pentecost" (Acts 20:16). Even as Paul was helping the church to grow as an institution, he realized the need to stay in touch with the fire and the wind, the source of the church's power and being.

That need continues in all traditions, in churches whose worship is ordered by prayer books and set liturgies as well as in churches who are "free" of them. Remember Marion, the character in Walker Percy's novel, *The Second Coming*, "who considered the interim prayer book an abomination." Marion Barrett clung to the printed page with which she was familiar as if it had been delivered once and for all from heaven, when in fact Thomas Cranmer compiled his first prayer book in 1549 as a "temporary form,"[49] from which in turn flowed "a long and noble line of Anglican Prayer Books," each attempting "to be relevant and useful instruments" for their particular time and place in history.[50]

Placing side by side these two different traditions, Anglican and Free Church, we discover that the continuing liveliness of any worshiping community is a function of something greater than its outward shape. Whatever the pattern of our prayers and praise—worship with a book or without a book—the vitality of the community's participation depends on periodically renewing the visions that gave us birth. The cloud tells us that we, like the apostle Paul hurrying to Jerusalem for Pentecost, must return to the wind and fire from which all true worship draws its life.

In our own day the cycle of fading congregational participation may repeat itself through the popularity of the electronic church. Many excellent things happen through television evangelism. People in nursing homes and hospitals appreciate the gospel beamed into their isolated rooms. Others whom the church has never reached hear the Word of God coming through the tube. But there is also the danger that the television screen could become like the rood screen in the medieval church or the raised platform in the nineteenth-century Free Church, a line of demarcation between the one who performs worship and the one who watches. Traveling on a plane to lead a worship workshop, we were told by the passenger next to us, "I like to watch church on television because that way I don't have to bother with other people."

Maybe that plane traveler was someone who would never darken the door of a church. But his understanding that worship is a performance seeps into our congregations. A pastor tells us, "My choir no longer wants to sit close to the congregation. They would like to do gospel music as if on a stage, 'The way it is on television' is how one of them explained it to me." Perhaps ages hence some writer on worship will record that during the era of the electronic church the balance between structure and spontaneity, clergy and congregation was lost again to rigid order and domination by the leadership. Perhaps that writer will record:

Gone — yet again! — were the people's prayers.
Gone — yet again! — were the people's responses.
Gone — yet again! — were the people's bread and wine.
Gone — yet again! — were the people's songs.

A question from the cloud: Is that how your church's worship will appear to those future generations looking back to you as their ancestors in the faith? Or will they see a balance between spontaneity and structure, clergy and congregation?

Soar with the Wind

Opening the Imagination to the Spirit

I once saw a small boy try to fly a kite on a windless day. He stood on a long, grassy stretch, laying out the tail, adjusting the bow of the crosspieces, and checking that the guide string had the right amount of slack. Then he bolted over the ground as fast as he could. The brilliant red kite climbed and climbed. The boy got to the end of the grass and stopped, and the kite fluttered to the ground. The boy wound his string around a stick and returned to study the kite. Again he checked the tail, the crosspieces, and the guide string. He weighed the kite in his hand, decided it was too heavy, and made the tail half as long. Once more he took off across the field, and the kite began to fly. But as soon as he stopped, it fluttered back to earth. Still not discouraged, he went through the same examination as before, this time increasing the bow in the crosspieces. He was bound and determined to get that kite up, and he obviously was an expert at how to adjust the thing for better flight. Yet again he poised himself on the edge of the grass, then charged across the field at full speed. The kite lifted higher! Then it made a papery, jiggling sound and swished to the ground. Another boy who had been watching called out, "You've got to wait for the wind."

"I know, I know," said the child winding up his string. But I could see in his face that he was greatly disappointed because he had to wait and because all of his skill could not compel the kite to soar up into the sky.

"You've got to wait for the wind." Those are hard words for a child and hard words for us adults too.[1] We tend to think that our efforts will ensure the success of what we do, and we bring this expectation to the planning of worship. We mistakenly believe there must be some surefire formula that will breathe life into our services. Yet we do not control God. The Holy Spirit is not a magic genie that we can conjure up by particular words and actions. Like the child with the kite and like the disciples before Pentecost (Acts 1) we too must wait for the wind of the Spirit.

Our waiting is not, however, empty time. The child adjusted the kite with all the intensity of mind that God had given him, and the disciples did not wait passively for the Spirit but "were constantly devoting themselves to prayer" (Acts 1:14). I have no doubt that, when the wind finally blew for that youngster, the kite lifted high into the sky even as "when the day of Pentecost had come . . . all of them were filled with the Holy Spirit" (Acts 2:1, 4).

We need then to be preparing for the Spirit so that our worship can soar with the wind. Like those disciples waiting between Christ's ascension and Pentecost, we must first of all devote ourselves with one accord to prayer. Unfortunately, our definition of prayer is often constricted and nebulous so that "preparation through prayer" sounds like a platitude, empty of any clear directive power.

For some of us prayer means a set form, perhaps in rhyme. We learn poem-prayers as children and never forget them. Maybe that is why we feel we are behaving improperly if we come to God mumbling incoherently. Much better, we think, to have a tried and orderly prayer, something worthy of the judging, parental God. This desire is as deep as the marrow in our bones and ancient as the disciples who asked their Master, "Lord, teach us to pray" (Luke 11:1).

Yet if we limit prayer to words, we seriously distort the basic concept. We reduce the possibilities for soaring with the Wind. A narrow verbal definition means that prayer occurs only when we use language or when we listen to someone else pray through words. Prayer would be confined to what is spoken or read or recited by memory. All of these can be powerful ways of praying. The very familiarity of the language helps some people to feel the closeness of the Spirit and their connection to the cloud of witnesses.

However, God comes to us through far more than words. God has not promised to answer the yearnings of our hearts exclusively through the syllables of human speech: "Likewise the Spirit helps us in our weakness; for we do not know how to pray as we ought, but that very Spirit intercedes for the saints according to the will of God" (Romans 8:26). If we want to soar with the wind of the Spirit, we must be ready for whenever and however the Spirit blows. Our prayer must be open to every form of call and response that passes between God and us.

Many worship traditions preserve this comprehensive understanding of prayer by applying the term to their entire liturgy, to what they sing and do as well as to their spoken address to God. For example, John Calvin called his Strassburg service "The Form of Church *Prayers.*" Thomas Cranmer put his liturgy in "The Book of Common *Prayer.*" The Puritans published "A booke of the Forme of Common *Prayers.*" And a classic work on black worship is titled "The *Prayer* Tradition of Black People." Despite outward differences in form and style, many worship traditions understand that worship is irreducibly prayer, irreducibly the call and response between God and us. There has been worship without reading from the Bible and worship without music and worship without sermons and worship without sacraments or ordinances and worship without buildings and worship without clergy but never worship without prayer in some form or fashion.

Worship is prayer.

And prayer is everything we do in response to God.

The early church stressed this action-oriented understanding by speaking of "doing" the worship service rather than "saying" it.[2] Thus when we prepare to soar with the wind, we call on every gift God has given us. We ask not only what we can say in worship but also what we can do. How can we worship God with all that God has made us to be?

Would a dance do it? A leap straight up as high as we could go and then another with outstretched arms and voice crying sounds of joy and release?

Would sitting with head tilted and eyes shut?

Would standing and singing the gladdest song we ever sang?

Would keeping perfect silence?

Would the enactment of a play?

Would reciting precious, ancient words?

Would standing around a table sharing bread and wine?

Would walking forward to give ourselves to Christ?

Would beating drums and blowing trumpets?

All of these actions and many more have been a part of the history of Christian worship, and all of them have been prayer, that fundamental dynamic of call and response between God and us.

Worship is prayer.

And prayer is everything we do in response to God.

These two principles are essential in preparing to soar with the wind. Lose sight of them and your worship will never get off the ground. But keep them always before you and there is no telling where and how the Spirit will lift the hearts of your congregation.

These two principles guide our ten-step process of worship preparation. The process is more than a method for engineering worship services. It is a spiritual discipline, a way of putting the church's comprehensive vision of prayer into practice, a way of devoting ourselves "with one accord to prayer."

We list the different steps in our discipline so that you can get a quick overview. Then we explore each in detail and help you understand how it works through examples from our own experience.

1. Define the situation, your congregation's hopes and needs.
2. Probe the treasures of Scripture and the cloud.
3. Identify the theme.
4. Decide what kind of service is appropriate.
5. Create an order of worship.
6. Make selections in light of the total liturgy.
7. Prepare adequately.
8. Make adjustments.
9. Worship God!
10. Evaluate.

Planning for community worship through this process is best done by those representing the community—the pastor, the musician, and people of various age groups, attitudes, organizations, and educational backgrounds in the church. These people bring a sense of the groups of which they are a part. They know how people in the congregation react to worship! During planning sessions, they bring their own ideas to the process as well as ideas from the groups they represent. Later on, they are able to explain to others the ideas upon which liturgical planning has been based.

Though usually it is not possible to gather this sort of advisory group every week, those doing the planning must make every effort to maintain strong communication with representative people so that concerns about worship may be expressed easily and often in all directions. This is an essential foundation to authentic corporate worship. How shall our liturgies be the people's prayer if planning is done without consulting the people? Like all foundations, this communication with the people must be carefully maintained. Slippage or deterioration in this basic area distorts all that rests upon it.

We are presenting the process in its fullest and ideal form. We do not mean to suggest that every church every week would create every service by following every step! Use our ten steps, not as a rigid system, but as a way of stirring your creativity and giving order to your preparation. Even when an individual plans alone, the steps can help in shaping the service to the community's needs.

Define the Situation

"I want to be sure to sing this hymn."

"I'd like to use my favorite Bible story."

"I once saw something in another church we ought to try."

"I'll be satisfied as long as what we do is not old and traditional.

"I'll be satisfied as long as what we do is not new and upsetting."

If a committee gathers with no more direction than the general purpose of "putting together a service," the chaos of the church in Corinth may reassert itself. The problem in all of the above ideas is that everyone of them begins with "I," with the singular world of the individual speaking rather than with the community of faith that will be worshiping. Worship is more than a pastiche of private opinions. In listening to the cloud we discovered that Peter and Paul did not follow their personal preferences but adapted their presentation of the gospel to the congregation.

Because worship belongs to all the people, we begin by defining the realities and needs of our faithful community. The other week, for example, I received a phone call from a pastor who was planning with her worship committee the dedication of a new church hall for Sunday school, social gatherings, volunteer organizations, and probably Sunday worship when it is too expensive to heat the sanctuary. She began by describing the congregation: "An active rural church trying to provide room not only for themselves but for groups from the larger community. Building has been quite a risk. But now it is done and people are excited about the possible use of the flexible space." Notice how we have not even begun to talk about the service. The very first thing we do is define the realities of the congregation. Yet many people plan worship without thinking precisely about the nature of the congregation. They assume, "I know that already." But often what they know is only what they see, think, and feel. Remember the exercise of taking a new location inside your church. How different things look when you sit in someone else's seat or stand where someone else stands!

The pastor on the phone continued, "We are going to have

an afternoon service at three o'clock. We have decided to hold it in the hall. The place is filled with light because it has loads of these big new thermal windows. There will be a table at one end spread with cookies and coffee, but otherwise the entire area is flexible; there is plenty of room for up to 120 folding chairs. We'll have to use the piano, an old upright in not too great a shape." A picture of the space, its possibilities and limitations, begins to form in my mind. I can hear the piano: rattling, untuned strings but still a support for the congregation's singing.

"The committee wants this service to be a joyful occasion. Like I said, the congregation really took a risk when they went ahead with this. But already the teachers are excited about it. The committee talked about reassuring people that it was right to take a risk and we want them to go out feeling that the building is part of the church's ministry to the rural area around them."

The minister does two things in these last comments; she gives me a feeling for the pastoral need of the congregation, the blend of anxiety, thanksgiving, and hope that people are bringing to the service. And she identifies in very specific terms how the service should function in the congregation's life; it should be a "joyful," "reassuring" occasion that helps them connect the building to the church's ministry.

Throughout the conversation I was impressed with the excellence of this minister's pastoral care. While she listens to the committee, she also gathers their insights into a clear, comprehensive statement of what is needed in the service. The balance between clergy and congregation is not slipping here. The pastor's sensitive leadership is keeping it finely tuned.

Of course, the need to define the situation was clearer in this case because I was not a member of the congregation and because the service was to be a special event. But the story highlights three essential issues that are present when we plan any worship and that taken altogether define the situation, even when they may not be immediately present to our awareness:

What are the realities with which we must work?

What pastoral needs are people bringing to worship?

How should the service function in the life of the congregation?

The way we view the realities with which we must work is as significant as what they are. If our attitude is "We cannot try anything new because we are stuck with this building or this choir or this congregation or . . . ," then, of course, there is nothing we can do. But if instead we ask, "What are the possibilities within the given limits of our space or choir or congregation or . . . ?", then we may be amazed at the openings God provides for the Spirit to blow among us. A thoughtful question expressed during worship planning may lead to possibilities never before examined. Consider the piano in the new church wing. The pastor described it as "an old upright in not too great a shape." The kite maker hears this as faint praise and asks, "Does it have to be like that?" "Old and upright" can be positive. What would it take to change "not too great a shape"?

It is exactly that sort of piano which had been used in our church's choir rehearsal room all the years that anyone could remember. When the tuner arrived to make some repairs one day, I asked about the future of the instrument.

"Nothing wrong with this piano," he said. "The hammers need filing and there are several adjustments which could improve things. But this is a good instrument. There's plenty of music still in it."

The cost of this work was equivalent to several tunings, but the piano now sounds gloriously robust. The atmosphere of serious effort has increased considerably in choir rehearsals since piano introductions and interludes no longer sound like rinky-dink parodies of music.

The wooden curlicues which had become unglued in the years of use are still missing from the outside of this piano and the tops of the keys are still discolored, but these items do not affect the piano's sound. We had taken as reality something which "did not have to be like that." We had assumed that change was impossible. Then a seemingly accidental conversation suggested the new reality.

Our role as worship leaders is to check the realities in our churches as closely as the child checked the crossbow and the tail of the kite. Perhaps the "old upright in not too great a shape" could be tuned for the dedication of the new wing. Perhaps someone in the congregaton would make the cost of the tuning a special gift to the church for this occasion. Perhaps reality is transformable! That is what a congregation in a snowbelt discovered when they moved their worship service from its airy sanctuary to the cellar during the winter. At first everyone was depressed at the thought of worshiping there. The underground room was a dull beige and had a low ceiling. But an industrial arts teacher in the congregation saw some new possibilities. He and the pastor gathered a committee during the summer which decided to paint the cellar a crisp white. Then the artist and some teenagers cut with a jigsaw four plywood panels into bold silhouettes of a dove, a burning bush, a chalice, and a loaf of bread. They painted each in bright but not electric colors. They arranged them on the walls and put a table in the midst of the room. (Can you hear the cloud chuckling at this story as they swap tales about house churches, basilicas, and cathedrals?)

The chairs in the cellar were old wooden ones that had been there as long as anyone could remember, ladder-backs with woven seats. In the former beige pallor of the room they had looked like relics, dingy and ready for the dump. But the bright walls brought out the earthy tones of the wood and the rush seats so that the chairs now lent a rich, warm feeling to the room. The cellar had been transformed into a space that invited the congregation to fellowship, prayer, and praise. And the entire project cost less than heating the sanctuary for one month during the dead of winter!

The story does not stop there. Several other things happened. Because the young people had helped with painting and designing the panels, they felt a greater investment in the worship of the church, and although a few members grumbled about leaving the beloved sanctuary—you will never please everyone—most of the congregation discovered a greater sense of community. What had first looked like a curse was a blessing—all because someone looked at a beige cellar with imaginary vision. Bring that vision to the realities of your congregation's life, and you will discover windows and doors that God is waiting for you to unlatch and open.

Sometimes, however, transformation is unlikely or impossible, and in that case it is better to face up to the reality than to fool ourselves with illusory expectations. For example, a choir of seven people cannot present an anthem for double chorus or sing a lengthy, triumphant work well. Seven people can present a shorter anthem in two or three voice parts very well. With a joyful spirit and a descanting instrument, that music could add greatly to the church's celebration on Sunday morning.

But the temptation is to forget the reality as we plan and to mistake our fantasies for real life.

Easter nears, and we plan the service that will come at the end of a long winter, looking forward to the declarations of victory, the fresh flowers, and the hymns of promise and strength sung by our church's people. Caught up in the spirit of all this, someone in the choir reports hearing a "tremendous" recording of a major choral work. "The words are perfect for Easter," we are told. "Let's get the music and have our choir sing it this year."

It is not easy to think realistically when all seven attentive faces are turned toward yours. Several had heard the same recording, for it had been broadcast on local radio late the night before. The thought of bringing that thrilling music to our congregation is very exciting. "They would be just as moved as we were," the singers are saying among themselves. Their eagerness to present this music is part of the reality. It should not be wasted. Yet that is exactly what may happen if the eagerness causes momentary amnesia and parts of reality are forgotten. The facts are:

There are only five weeks until Easter.

The new music must be ordered, delivered, and learned.

And two of us don't read music very well.

Two others may miss rehearsals because of business trips.

One other person remembers, but can hardly bear to mention it, that a family reunion will take him to the West Coast on Easter weekend.

Eagerness could alter some of these realities. Perhaps it would move the choir to agree to invest extra rehearsal time in preparing to sing the work they had found so attractive. But the precious eagerness is only one part of an equation which is far better resolved in planning than on Easter Sunday morning. Here leadership must rise to its own essential role. We must name reality: seven (six) people will probably be frustrated, angered, and ultimately disappointed by their efforts to reproduce the music sung by a large choir on that beautiful recording. The leader who has special gifts in music must anticipate that fact, state it clearly, and then immediately begin working to find music of a similar character which could be successfully presented by the six singers. Furthermore, the reality may be strengthened by naming it with a graceful name. The search shall not be for a "substitute" anthem for a small choir. We shall be looking instead for a suitable anthem of a delicate texture, something which will bring out the best abilities of the vocal ensemble.

Even when the realities with which we must work are fixed, the pastoral needs of a congregation keep shifting. People do not bring the same expectations to every service. Their anticipation varies with the church year and with the rhythms of joy and tragedy and everyday work that mark their lives. People do not look for the first Sunday in Lent to ring with the ecstatic carolings of Easter morning nor do they carry the same hope and belief into the sanctuary Sunday after Sunday. One week I will bring doubt to the service and you will bring faith. But the next week I may bring faith and you will bring doubt. One week I will bear need and you will bear a heart full of thanks. But the next week I may bear the thankful heart and you the need. One week I will come in joy and you in sorrow. And that is only you and me. Consider the entire congregation—the multiplicity of belief and doubt, needs and thanks, joy and sorrow that meet when we all gather together.

Effective worship planning braids together two strands of time, the church year and the seasons of life that are peculiar to the local congregation, not only the personal rhythms of doubt and faith but also the ebb and flow of the community's activities. These vary a great deal from congregation to congregation. Suburban churches often tend to be quieter during the summer months with their most rigorous schedules beginning in September while many city churches surge with activity as soon as school lets out.

Plot a graph of your church year, using one line for the seasons and festivals of faith and another for the unique flow of your congregation's life. Indicate central festive occasions, for example, Easter, and list below them the special expectations that people bring to those services. Then do the same for those events that are unique to your congregation. Use the chart to discover if there are any important Christian festivals that you slight. For example, Pentecost used to be a joyful celebration in the early church. We have already seen how Paul hurried back to Jerusalem to be there in time for Pentecost (see page 74). Reclaiming that ancient festival offers possibilities for soaring with the wind of the Spirit even as the disciples did. Also, use your chart to visualize how any one service is not an isolated act of worship but is part of an ongoing discipline of prayer and praise.

Sensitivity to the highs and lows of the church year inevitably leads us to ask: How should the particular service we are planning function in the life of the congregation? "We want them to go out feeling that the building is part of the church's ministry to the rural area around them," said the minister on the phone describing her committee's hope for the dedication service. Notice how specific the statement of the goal is. Sometimes worship leaders veer away from being so explicit because they fear becoming "manipulative." They do not want to use people's emotions like the strings of a marionette, and in this they are absolutely right. We must always honor the integrity of the human soul. Therefore, when we ask how a service should function, we do not mean: How will it compel a particular response from people? But rather: How will it fit into the overall pattern of the church's ministry?

Will the service strengthen the sense of community?

or

Express a special grief or hope?

or

Renew our personal commitment to Christ?
   or
Set us on a journey of preparation for a future event?
   or
   . . . ?

Every service functions at several different levels of meaning. But clarity about the primary function alerts us to our special needs as we move through the process of preparation.

Probe the Treasures of Scripture and the Cloud

I am still on the phone with the pastor planning the dedication service. We are probing the treasures of Scripture and the cloud for resources that will match the church's need and that may figure prominently in the service. "Flexible, real, alive" people have dedicated buildings in the past, and we need to listen to their witness.

I reflect with the pastor: "The first thing that comes to mind is Solomon dedicating the temple and the beautiful prayer he offered that the temple would be a house of prayer. You might want to use his prayer as yours or use it as a model for yours."

The word "house" touches off another chain of associations: "There's also the psalm that opens, 'Unless the Lord builds the house, those who build it labor in vain.' You might have the congregation sing it or there may be a special anthem on the text. And then there's also a passage in which King David expresses the feeling that he should build God a house since he now lives in a splendid house of cedar while the Lord dwells in a tent. God has a great response. The gist of it is something like: 'You won't build me a house; I'll build you a house. I don't need a house to dwell in. I've done fine tenting with you. It's you and your people who need the house.' There is a pun in the Hebrew on 'house' meaning both 'building' and 'family,' something like the 'household of faith,' I believe, but you better check that."

"That relates to what we were talking about in the committee, 'Who's the building for?' "

"You might also trace the words 'house' and 'temple' in a concordance and see how they are used in different contexts.

That may help you connect the building to the church's ministry—especially those New Testament passages in which Christ
is referred to as the foundation or chief cornerstone. You might
be able to write a litany for the ceremony of dedication that
draws on the imagery of a living temple from Ephesians 2."

Notice what is happening in the conversation. We have started
with what immediately comes to mind, a possible parallel between Solomon's temple dedication and the church dedication,
but we do not stop there. We follow the associations of words
and concepts which that initial idea touches off. Our process,
tracing the net of images woven by the cloud through the centuries, is based on the insight of John Donne (1572–1631), one
of the greatest poets and preachers in the English language:

> But thou art also (*Lord* I intend it to thy *glory*, and let no *prophane
> misinterpreter* abuse it to thy *diminution*) thou art a *figurative*, a
> *metaphoricall God too*: A *God* in whose words there is such a height
> of *figures*, such *voyages*, such *peregrinations* to fetch remote and
> precious *metaphors* . . . O what words but thine, can expresse the
> inexpressible *texture* and *composition* of thy *word*. . . .[3]

How will the "texture and composition" of God's Word be
known at 3 o'clock on Sunday afternoon when that rural congregation gathers in their new hall with the thermal windows,
a table stacked with cookies, and a piano in not too great shape?
How will the texture and composition of God's word be known
whenever we gather to worship? That is the guiding question
as we probe the treasures of Scripture and the cloud. Sometimes
the biblical texts are already given. If your church is following
a lectionary, then that is one of the realities which defines your
situation. Unlike the service of dedication or other special events,
you do not need to search for a biblical focus. However, you do
need to probe the treasures that are in the text. One way, probably the best known, is to use Bible study aids, such as com-
mentaries, various translations, and Bible dictionaries. Such
work is essential, but we have discovered that in itself this
approach is inadequate. Used alone, it tends to result in services
that are too dry. It is like a doctor who runs every test on you
but has never talked with you as a person. You are more than
a biological specimen. You are a "flexible, real, alive" person

who needs to be understood as a physical-psychological whole. Likewise, a biblical text represents the faith of "flexible, real, alive" people and there is no way you can get into the full reality of it through analysis alone. You need to pray your way in and through and around the text.

Remember: worship is prayer.

John Donne knew this. He and other religious poets of his day used a method of meditation in which they stepped into a biblical passage much as we stepped into the Rembrandt picture. Imagining ourselves a character in a text is a soulful way to probe the treasures of Scripture and the cloud, perhaps even a necessary way. For we cannot help the congregation touch and taste "the inexpressible texture and composition" of God's word if we have not touched and tasted that truth ourselves.

Here is an example of the process at work. The gospel text for the worship service is the healing of the bleeding woman in Luke 8. Before thinking of a sermon or a hymn or a responsive reading or any other liturgical element, the first thing I need to know is how this story is true now for me and for the congregation. If there is no authentic witness to the healing power of Jesus Christ, the most beautiful music and the most perfectly executed worship service is worthless. Therefore, I probe the gospel story by becoming the bleeding woman,

feeling the weight of my illness,
the sapping of my vital energy,
the rejection by a society hostile to women, doubly hostile to bleeding women,
the bitterness of spending all my money on physicians who failed me,
the desperate lunge in a crowd to touch Jesus' garment,
and oh, the wonder! of Christ's healing power flowing into me.

Tears roll down my face as I feel the bleeding stop. I do not yet know how the worship service will witness to Christ's miraculous power. All I know is that power has entered my mind and body and there is an irresistible urge to witness to it. But I will not trust my experience alone. The story is the community's story, not just mine. Therefore, when we are planning the service, I will invite the other members of the worship committee to step into the text. Perhaps the healing power of Christ will awaken a flow of melody in the musician that can help the entire congregation reach for Christ. Or maybe one of the lay people will see a connection between the healing and some untold wound from the church's past that I have not been aware of but which needs to be touched. Who knows where this process will lead? I do not, but I trust the Spirit to lead us into the truth that is greater than any of our private worlds. I do not become prematurely anxious about getting down the details of the service because it is important to give God time to work upon everyone who has leadership responsibility for the worship. This will not only raise greater riches out of our imaginations, but it will also influence the very way we conduct the service. When Holy Truth has touched people, it has an undeniable impact on their voices, their eyes, and their body language. We sense a genuineness of conviction that can never be drummed up because it comes from the marrow of the bones and the center of the heart.

So far we have used only the Bible, but do not forget the vast cloud of witnesses who have collected, shaped, preserved, translated, passed on, and celebrated the Scriptures through art, song, and worship for two thousand years. Rembrandt shows us dimensions and shadings of the gospel which we would miss without the guidance of his eye. John Donne's poetry draws us into the reality of the "figurative, a metaphorical God." Black slaves, known by name to God though not to us, identify the murmurings of our souls through the genius of their song. And the list goes on and on and on. Far too often in planning worship we use the Bible as a boundary for what we do rather than as the measure of what we do. A boundary indicates: "Stop here." But a measure indicates: "Check to see if what you are using is up to the standard." The Bible is our measure, not our boundary. We listen to the cloud of witnesses without whom we would miss many of the greatest treasures from the Scriptures. We are like those people who constructed the middle and upper walls of the cathedrals. They were building on top of foundations laid by masons who had died generations before.[4] In a similar fashion, when we plan worship, we are taking our place in "the household of God, built upon the foundation of the apostles and prophets, with Christ Jesus himself as the cornerstone. In him the whole structure is joined together and grows into a holy temple in the Lord; in whom you also are built together spiritually into a dwelling place for God" (Ephesians 2:19*b*–22).

Identify the Theme

God is mysterious but not obscure. It is a mystery that God would come to live among us on this tiny speck of matted mud hurtling through the immensities of space, a mystery the church can never stop singing, praying, and proclaiming. But it is not obscure. It is as clear as the sunniest day at high noon that God loves us. And we must never justify worship that obscures God by an appeal to the mystery of the divine. For that cheapens the wonder and the glory of who God is.

Sometimes people like to contrast clarity and mystery, to suggest that they are opposites. But in fact they are intimately related. The greater the clarity the greater the mystery. If you want people to know more of the mystery of God in worship, clarify the theme and mood of your services. If you ask people to focus on the entirety of God, you will muddle their minds and God will appear obscure. But if you invite them to explore a particular dimension of the gospel, they will be filled with awe at the wonder of God.

Identifying the theme of a service involves more than isolating a concept from the Bible or singling out a need from the congregation. We discover the theme by looking at the community's life in light of God's Word. The theme is God's revelation to our local congregation, not to some idealized abstraction called THE CHURCH. We ask what is God saying through
    this text,
      this music,
        this season,
          this picture,
            this poem,
              this event
                to us?

We weave back and forth between our immediate situation as a congregation and the witness that is coming to us from Scripture and the cloud. If we were getting ready to dedicate the new church wing which the pastor phoned about, we would hold a planning session in the hall itself. We would read aloud some of the passages we were considering and study the building. What is God's living Word for the people who will be gathering in this place? We do not rush to answer the question out of the busyness of our own minds, but we wait silently for the Spirit to speak. To center our hearts, we focus our mental energies on the building through a simple phrase: "nails and wood."

Nails and wood.

Nails and wood.

Nails and wood.

We want to know how God is speaking through the nails and wood for which persons in this congregation have poured out their gifts of money and time.

Nails and wood.

I think of the carpenters who put the hall together.

Carpenters! Christ was a carpenter.

The Spirit is beginning to move, to tug on the thread of meaning that hems together the ancient witness and the immediate situation so that I feel its pull in my own heart.

Nails and wood.

My soul constructs from these two plain words a prayer:

Nails and wood, Creator God, have long been part of your story.

Solomon brought cedars from Tyre for the temple.

And we name as our Lord a carpenter from Nazareth.

Thank you for more than the tables and chairs he hammered together.

Thank you for his carpentry work on hearts and minds and souls.

Nails and wood.

They were part of your story on Good Friday.

The carpenter was crucified with the tools of his trade.

Nails and wood.

They are part of your story in this our new church hall.

We want to praise you and serve you through this building.
May it be a sign to the world that despite the nails and wood
   of the cross,
Jesus Christ still swings a hammer for love and faith and hope.
In his name. Amen.

The Spirit is materializing the theme through our total process
of immersion in Scripture, reflecting on the situation, and waiting upon the Lord. We might or might not use the specific
prayer which has formed in our soul—that decision comes later
in the process—but we share it with the committee in order to
help them clarify what God is saying to the church.

Seldom does the theme of a service simply spring to mind,
and when it does, we often discover that it gets redefined
through our preparation. For example, during Lent one year
our choir mustered all of its energy for a major project: singing
J. S. Bach's Cantata No. 3, *O God, How Many Pains of Heart*. We
decided that instead of presenting a special concert, we would
make the cantata the sermon during a regular service. The minister would introduce the preacher for the day, J. S. Bach, with
the musicians offering brief musical illustrations from the work
to prepare the community for active rather than passive listening. The cantata would thus become the congregation's worship,
rather than a performance by a few for the many.

Studying the text and score, we decided that the theme was
"progress on the spiritual journey." We began to choose lessons,
hymns, and prayers so that the entire congregation could frame
the choir's contribution with related acts of praise. But the living
Spirit of God stirred up different meanings in the choir room.
Each rehearsal was unfolding the wonders of the composition.
Many times after singing a musical phrase just as they wished,
hushed silence would fall upon the choir. They knew they were
in the presence of the divine Word and the Word was not
"progress on the spiritual journey," but some other theme struggling to be enunciated. We scrapped our original service ideas.
We knew it was more important to listen to the Spirit than to
clutch our preconceptions of what God was saying to us. Working together as joint interpreters of the Word of God, music
director and minister finally recognized the fundamental mes-

sage of the Spirit speaking through text and music to our congregation: "The faithful Christian encounters challenges daily which only prayerful reliance on God will countermand." The basic dynamic of the music was not a journey forward but a seesawing action between doubt and belief, sorrow and hope, temptation and faithfulness. The shape and content of the congregation's worship would need to reflect that struggle if it were to be integrated effectively with the cantata. A key phrase in the final chorale, "Guard my heart, O God," helped us make decisions about responses, prayers, and readings and led to the writing of a litany which drew together the total experience of choir and congregation interacting:

When doubt threatens to drown my faith,
Guard my heart, O God.
When despair begins to destroy my hope,
Guard my heart, O God.
When bitterness keeps me from forgiving,
Guard my heart, O God.
When temptation beckons me from your will,
Guard my heart, O God.
When hate burns more fiercely than love,
Guard my heart, O God.
When my commitment to Jesus Christ wavers,
Guard my heart, O God.
From this day forth and forevermore. Amen.

The litany followed immediately after the cantata. The congregation prayed the response, "Guard my heart, O God," in a tone of sacred awe, as if the choir's music were now singing in their own hearts. The special offering of the musicians was thus transformed into the worship of all the people.

Even when the choir's role is less prominent, there is a profound need for musicians and pastors to listen and interpret the Spirit together. It does no good to identify the theme in words or music if each is at cross-purposes with the other. We think here of a pastor who one Sunday offered a reflective, meditative sermon in response to a request from some members of the congregation. The anthem that day, which followed the pastor's message on hearing God in soft and silent ways, featured kettle drums and a trumpet! The choir director was not deliberately sabotaging the service. The two of them simply had not talked with each other. On another Sunday the drums and trumpet might have lifted the hearts of the entire congregation, but on this occasion those festive instruments stirred up spiritual confusion in the congregation which the pastor saw reflected in their faces. God seemed obscure rather than mysterious because those responsible for worship had not worked together to clarify the theme and mood of the service. Consider how gloriously different things might have been if they had consulted each other. One week the congregation might have gone out listening as never before to those caverns of the heart which are usually inaudible to their busy minds. Another week they might have returned home with faith echoing like drums and trumpets inside them. And they would have known more completely the fullness of God. The carefully planned variations in worship over time would have made them more open to glory.

Decide What Kind of Service Is Appropriate

Before getting ready for a party, people want to know what kind of occasion it will be. A question about what to wear may express the deeper concern of what bearing and attitude they should bring to the event. If the host says it will be a formal affair but appears in casual dress, the guests may be disoriented, perhaps even upset, because of the discontinuity between the expectation and the reality.

Worship, as we observed in chapter 2, is a party given by a host who supplies the most important things—Spirit, strength, mercy, hope—but who leaves the details to us. God is depending on our hospitality. We must decide what is appropriate to the particular theme we are celebrating. The themes of faith are not neutral truths that can be ornamented according to whim. There is a tone to any theme which is part of its character and which awakens certain expectations in the congregation. If we violate those expectations, the worshipers will not be able to join in the spirit of the occasion.

Sometimes we are tempted to view a congregation's expectations negatively, as their defense mechanism against trying anything new. If we take this perspective, then our worship leadership turns sour. Either we begrudgingly "give them what they want" or we righteously insist on "doing things our way." Both strategies spell doom for a church's worship life.

However, there is another way of understanding the situation: people's expectations reveal that they take worship seriously. If they had a smaller personal investment in what happens, then they would not be upset by worship which they considered inappropriate to the theme. Their expectations indicate that they are preparing themselves as thoughtfully as the guest who asks if the supper will be formal or informal.

Deciding what kind of service is appropriate involves building positively on worshipers' expectations without being limited in every detail. This is exactly what two pastors did in a church several years ago when they tried a different kind of service during Holy Week. For as long as anyone could remember, every Maundy Thursday the congregation had celebrated the Last Supper in the church's sanctuary. People had deep and sacred memories of that service, expecting always to hear a favorite member of the choir sing, "Were You There When They Crucified My Lord?" Because nearly everyone in the congregation worked and could not get free on Good Friday, they usually made a special effort to attend that evening. This particular year the pastors along with the worship committee decided that instead of the usual service in the sanctuary, they would hold a simple meal in the church hall. They would follow this with worship modeled after the services of Tenebrae (Latin for "shadows") that go back at least to the twelfth century.

When the first announcement was made, there were immediate complaints, all of them centering on the sacredness of Maundy Thursday. Pastors and worship committee affirmed this expectation and explained that the Tenebrae service was an attempt to deepen our sense of wonder and thanks for Christ's sacrifice. The church would not be denying tradition but claiming more of it. Many people were satisfied with this interpretation and many were not.

Maundy Thursday came, and attendance was markedly down from previous years. The service was simple, as was the tradition in the sanctuary. After the meal, the congregation remained seated around the tables and all lights were turned out except for twelve candles spread throughout the hall. The service began with a hymn that people knew by heart, followed by the reading of the penitential psalm and the Lord's Supper. Then twelve members of the congregation read the passion narrative in sequence. After each passage, the reader blew out the candle before him or her and there was a period of silence. Eventually the room was totally dark and still. Then the beloved choir member sang "Were You There When They Crucified My Lord?" and the service concluded with a benediction and the lighting of a single candle to represent the hope of the resurrection.

Many worshipers wept. All of them agreed that their fears had been misplaced, and the next year, before Lent had arrived, church members—including those who stayed away but heard about the service from others—were saying, "I hope we'll have the Tenebrae service again." The church did, and this time it was packed, a larger congregation than had ever assembled on Maundy Thursday in the sanctuary. Two years later, people were looking forward to "our traditional Tenebrae service."

The story illustrates that appropriateness is a function of something larger than liturgical details, as important as those sometimes are. The worship committee exercised the finest possible leadership. To decide what kind of service is appropriate, they did not ask, "Will everyone like it?" Instead, the committee honored the essential expectations of the congregation while designing a service that maintained the integrity of the theme. We are sure there must have been some few people who never were—and never would be—pleased with what happened. But the vast majority of that congregation grew in their knowledge and love of Christ because the worship committee had arrived at a profound understanding of what was appropriate for their particular community.

The Maundy Thursday service we have described may or may not fit into your congregation's life, but the principles of appropriateness can be translated to any situation:

What are the essential expectations of the congregation?

What is the tone of our theme?

What kind of service will effectively blend together these concerns?

We ask these questions to clarify our minds, and we turn to
God to untangle the perplexity of heart and soul that lies beyond
the reach of our rational process:

How shall we worship you, O God?

You are holy.
We are common.
You are Spirit.
We are flesh.
You are eternal.
We are momentary.
Heaven is so far from earth
we may mask the soul in icy reverence
and make our praise too formal.

Yet you know what it is to be human,
to have a heart of muscle
and a frame of bone,
to be born
and to grow up,
to suffer
and to die.
Heaven is so close to earth
we may mask the soul in chummy talk
and make our praise too folksy.

How shall we worship you, O God?

In many ways!
In exalted speech
for truth beyond our reach.
In prayer that's blunt and plain
to question death and pain.
In melody and song
to make the weak heart strong.
In dance, in steps of joy and grace
to move our praise through time and space.

And having spoken, sung, and danced,

We shall be still and know that you are God—
Before the word was on our tongue,
you spelled it with your lips;
Before the song had left our lungs,
you hummed it high in heaven;
Before the dance was in our bodies,
the beat was in your heart.
Amen.[5]

Create an Order of Worship

Every church organizes its worship according to some pattern, whether kept in a prayer book or printed on a bulletin or passed on by example. And every service depends on that order, even those services which depart from it since in that case the community explains the difference in light of "the way we usually worship." Therefore, when we create an order of service, we never start with a blank tablet, as if the community did not already have a common understanding of what should happen when it gathers. That is a critical weakness in much so-called "experimental worship." It forgets the context of the community's understanding and thereby tears the fabric of tradition and continuity that is essential to every church's identity.

Creative worship at its best expands and deepens tradition, sometimes through the imaginative adaptation of its regular liturgical pattern. We often fail to see the possibilities in our regular orders of worship because we approach them like a fill-in-the-blank exercise: "Choose the hymns. Put in a prayer. List the Scripture readings. Give the sermon title. Get the anthem from the choir director." But consider the possibilities if, instead of treating each of these as a separate item, we start examining their interrelationships and how each can help the other to unfold God's revelation to the community. For example, how might the prayers draw on the language and imagery of the Scripture readings? Maybe the sermon is going to center on the Old Testament lesson. What then about the reading from the gospel? It may not fit in the sermon without forcing and damaging the text. But there may be a way of using the lesson to structure a prayer which will help people to step into the Good

News of Jesus Christ. Remember the exercise with the story of the bleeding woman? (See pages 91-92.) Out of that immersion in the text we created the following prayer as a way of touching some profound pastoral needs that could not be covered in the sermon:

We bleed.
We bleed, O Christ, from the inner wounds of
grief, guilt, and grudges
that cut the soul and drain the spirit.
We have tried all the standard remedies:
  "Forget it."
  "Keep yourself busy."
  "Think about other things."
But Band-Aids cannot stop internal bleeding.
Today we reach for you, O Christ.
We do not know you well enough to take your hand,
and we would be embarrassed to have the world see our need
    for you.
So we, like the bleeding woman in the gospel,
will be content to touch the fringe of your garment,
to let the boundary of your being brush the boundary of ours.
We believe, Lord,
  that the slightest pressure of your forgiveness
  stops the hemorrhage of guilt,
  that the gentlest touch of your presence
  reduces the flow of grief,
  that the application of your grace
  heals our grudges.
We reach for you, Christ. Amen.[6]

This prayer was the only innovation in the service. It was offered as a meditation on the gospel text with adequate pauses to let people enter the healing story with their own needs. Months later several worshipers revealed that they were still continuing the prayer in their own way and that they felt Christ was healing them. We soared with the wind that Sunday because we asked one simple question: How will the prayers and the Scripture readings be related?

Or think of the possibilities that begin to multiply if the worship leaders and music director regularly consult about the theme and mood of the service. Instead of the anthem serving as a disconnected interlude or as camouflage for the offering, it could be an integral part of the sermon, completing through melody the truth that can only be partially presented through words alone. I once heard an inspiring sermon on the battle of Jericho which was immediately followed by the choir's hand-clapping, foot-stomping rendition of "Joshua Fought the Battle of Jericho." Years later the sermon—on God's power to tumble down our walls—is still rumbling in my heart because I can hear that choir singing even though the exact words of the preacher have faded from memory. What wise, wise worship leaders that choir director and minister were. They knew how to help a church soar with the wind.

None of these changes requires rebuilding the universe, although that is often how awesome a task revitalizing worship seems. All we have done is ask: What new possibilities do we see in our regular pattern of worship when we consider the service as an integrated whole? Worship leaders who use this question to enrich a church's regular liturgy will collect a reservoir of trust and appreciation in the congregation from which they can draw in trying more innovative services.

Creating a new order of worship draws us into the primordial process of bringing order out of chaos: "In the beginning God created the heavens and the earth. The earth was without form and void, and darkness was upon the face of the deep; and the Spirit of God was moving over the face of the waters" (Genesis 1:1-2). "In the beginning" for us means that nebulous and sometimes scary moment when the worship committee first gathers together. Feelings, ideas, needs, and hopes float through the committee at random. They are "without form and void." Then the group offers a prayer for their work, and they begin defining the situation. It is not immediately clear what world will come to birth, but the Spirit of God is moving over the face of the committee's waters as people exchange their perceptions and ideas. The next three stages—probing the treasures, identifying the theme, deciding what kind of service is appropriate—are like the opening days of creation; they separate out the primary realities, the light from the darkness, the waters above and below the firmament, the dry land from the sea. The committee is creating the boundaries and general shape of the service. People may make many specific suggestions—a hymn, a prayer, a reading, an action, a drama, a posture, a picture—but while everyone of them is recorded, none is finally settled upon.

By now we have arrived at the fifth stage, "Creating an order of worship," although everything we have done so far might come under that general heading. We have been working as a committee of the whole. Like all committees, however, there comes a point at which the group process becomes a less efficient way of handling the task, and those with special skills are asked to develop a program based on the community's contributions. The role of the worship leaders here is not unlike that of the architect for a medieval cathedral. The architect drew up a plan that incorporated the gifts of many artisans—quarry workers, masons, carpenters, sculptors, glassmakers, roofers, and blacksmiths. Each supplied something vital and precious; yet they looked to the architect to design a building that would be grander than a mere conglomeration of their independent gifts.

In a similar fashion, the role of the worship leaders is to draw the contributions of the entire committee into a coherent and aesthetically pleasing order of service. This requires both openness to the group's ideas and a willingness to make judgments based on sound knowledge of music, theology, and tradition. Far from diminishing the role of pastors and musicians, this process requires a high degree of professional and pastoral skill from the church's leadership.

There are generally two ways to formulate the order of service. In some cases the order almost presents itself naturally. For example, a service using the monologues for the Rembrandt etching (see pages 15-23) developed directly from a conversation with the worship committee of a Baptist church which had invited me to lead a series of services to renew their congregational life and to empower them to reach out to the surrounding community. At the first meeting I did the listening and they did the talking. I asked a few questions, but they were all aimed at a single goal: "Defining the situation." I went away with an image of a diverse community that covered a spectrum of belief, from devout Christians to seekers and skeptics. Next I listened to the cloud to discover a treasure that might give us a focus. I settled on the Rembrandt etching which I brought back to the committee several weeks later. I then invited them to step into the picture, just as you did earlier in this book. When we talked about what the committee experienced, the conversation moved from the periphery of the picture to the center, following primarily the four characters whose thoughts I have recorded in the monologues.

We next tried to summarize what happened by stating a theme. This took more than an hour. I came up with the final phrase, but the words and concepts were drawn from the group:

Stepping into Jesus' Story
and Finding a Place in His Family.

The flow of the conversation presented us with a natural order for the introductory service; we would move from skepticism through legalism and reticent faith to fervent discipleship. I now met with the pastor and music director alone to work out precise selections and actions which would pull together the many contributions of the larger group. Some of the language in the monologues was tailored to fit the lyrics of the anthems and solos. For example, I gave the skeptic in the floppy hat the repeated line, "Is it real?" because we had a superb soloist who was going to sing a gospel song with the refrain, "It's real." Thus music and monologue would be an integrated dramatic unit. Note here how group discussion and musical selection decided the content of the "sermon." Preachers often fail to see many creative possibilities for worship because they always start first from their sermons. Do not get trapped in this pattern. It is too narrow an approach to the Word of God and often prevents the church from soaring with the wind.

Rembrandt's picture had given order to the committee's conversation which in turn became the order of the service. This pattern of the structure emerging through the process often repeats itself whenever the leaders start with a specific treasure from the cloud, whether it is a piece of visual, musical, or literary art or a particular passage of Scripture, as in an Easter service we developed at our seminary. The academic year was winding down, and the seniors expressed a need to say good-bye, to face the tensions of the future, and to be sent out on their witness to the gospel—all of this while celebrating the resurrection of Christ. The worship committee could not gather because the students were too involved in final papers and exams, just as in the local church there are seasons when you are not able to meet. So we prepared the service on our own but kept in mind how the students had defined the situation. We reread the resurrection stories and settled on the road to Emmaus story (Luke 24:13-35) because it seemed to fit with the forces driving through our community. There is both the despair of the disciples as they begin their walk and the flame in their hearts of meeting the risen Lord. We decided the entire service would lead the congregation to recognize the risen Lord in their lives.

We found the order of worship uncoiling effortlessly out of the text. Each section of the biblical story would be recounted in simple sentences as an introduction to the liturgical action which interprets it. We hoped that using the text in this manner would reflect in spirit the way it functioned in the primitive church. Before Luke recorded the story, it was probably modified by the community's worship, by the early practice of blessing and breaking bread together. Our service would claim that tradition by sharing bread when we came to verse 30: "When he was at the table with them, he took bread, blessed and broke it, and gave it to them."

Persons in the congregation would be invited to recount resurrection stories from their time during seminary, thus allowing seniors a chance to recount something significant from their careers at the school while keeping the focus on the Easter season.

We talked extensively about the music, especially about the need for it to change in mood from despair to the joy and confidence of the resurrection. We decided to put the reading of the text prior to the organ prelude so that the sad introductory music could be a medium of meditation that would move the people into the opening tone of the service. The final hymn tune, Duke Street, is a bold, beloved melody that leads the congregation to sing the closing Easter lyrics with confidence. Likewise, the postlude carries on the exuberant note of faith that characterizes the end of the Emmaus story.

We wrote special unison prayers of confession and commissioning that grew directly out of the flow of the service. This is a way of helping the congregation pray their way into the New Testament story, not unlike John Donne and the other seventeeth-century English poets who meditated their way inside the Scriptures.

Worship for the Season of Easter

"And their eyes were opened and they recognized him."

Prelude in Words: Luke 24:13-35
Prelude in Music: "Come, Savior of the People"   J. S. Bach

We Share Our Doubt and Despair

Walking the Emmaus Road (*An invitation to join the two disciples*)
Hymn: "I lift Up My Soul"

A Stranger Joins Us

Are you not aware? (*A meditation on our blindness to Christ*)
Prayer of Confession:

Lord Christ, forgive us.
We have seen you but not recognized you.
Our eyes were blinded:
By doubt.
By despair.
By fear.
By loneliness.
By hate.
Yet you were with us.
In the stranger.
In the listening ear.
In the kind word.
In the shared meal.
Open our eyes today.
Prepare us to recognize you.
In the broken bread.

In the people gathered around your table.
And send us to tell the world:
"The Lord has risen indeed." Amen.

The Stranger Listens and Interprets Our World

The congregation shares resurrection stories.

The Stranger Shares a Meal with Us

Hymn: "Let Us Break Bread Together"
Sharing the loaf from the Emmaus Table (*The congregation breaks bread together.*)

We Run to Tell the World

Prayer of Commissioning (*First in silence, then in unison*):
Lord Christ, our hearts are on fire with you.
We will share the story of your listening
—that the lonely may find a friend.
We will share the story of your teaching
—that the lost may find a purpose.
We will share the story of your healing
—that the blind may see and the lame walk.
We will share the story of your dying
—that the suffering may feel your presence.
We will share the story of your rising
—that the world may serve its king. Amen.

Hymn: "Christ Is Alive"   Duke Street
Benediction
Postlude: "Christ Lay in Death's Bands"   J. S. Bach

That is the order of worship as it was shaped by the New Testament text and the pastoral needs of the community. Although first offered in our seminary community, we know of several churches that have adapted this service to their own situations, and it has been warmly received by both traditionalists and innovators.

Why?

We believe it is because there is a basic biblical integrity to the service. The order is not something contrived. It is not difference for difference's sake. Rather, it flows from a resurrection experience that reaches across the ages of Christian faith, from the early church to the present day.

However, not every new order of worship presents itself with the ease of the Rembrandt and Emmaus services. Sometimes the worship committee meets and there is a torrent of ideas but not one firm piece of ground on which to stand and get our bearings. This tends to be the case whenever we are groping to define a real but elusive need.

"People need help with prayer," observed a worship committee member at one of our meetings. "I do not know exactly what I have in mind, but it would be a service that would help people experience what prayer is about." That honest statement of perplexity touched off a conversation which lasted for about an hour. During that time we made no attempt at deciding what to do liturgically. Instead, we kept trying to clarify what each of us means by prayer, how it functions in our personal lives, and how we see it as part of our community life. When we began to shift the conversation from "defining the situation," the group was not able to move clearly into either of the next two stages—probing the treasure or identifying the theme—but there was a consensus about the fourth stage, about what kind of service would be appropriate: the service should take place in a room where we could arrange ourselves in a circle to strengthen our sense of the community's role in prayer. And the service would invite the congregation to try a number of different postures for prayer—standing, sitting, kneeling—as a way of engaging the entire person. We talked quite a while about how this might feel threatening to some people; then we decided that if each posture was related to the theme and modeled by a worship leader, the congregation could join in without feeling awkward.

That is as far as the committee was able to go. As worship leaders we were left with what seemed like an enormous task: creating an order of worship from a myriad of ideas and feelings. But our job proved easier than it first appeared. We turned to a concordance and traced the word "prayer" in light of our wide-ranging discussion. We looked up a helpful article on "postures" in a worship dictionary,[7] and within an hour the cloud was filling us with ideas. We organized the service by thinking of a series of concentric circles, each one leading outward to a larger concept of prayer. The service opened with reflections on private prayer, then moved to consider prayer among the community of believers, and ended with prayers for the entire world. The verbal content was mirrored by our bodies. We started with eyes shut and head bowed, and we concluded with all standing and lifting their hands and eyes toward heaven while the four worship leaders offered this benediction:

We pray with our arms stretched out to embrace the world.
With our eyes open and expectant to see you, Lord.
With our hands ready to heal and to hold.
With our feet ready to run where you need us.
For Christ's sake, Amen.

The next week we gathered in the sanctuary worshiping "the way we usually do." But it was not exactly the same. It never is after we have tried another order of service, for we return to our usual pattern with a heightened awareness of the riches and meaning of our tradition. Sometimes this leads to a permanent outward change in the way we do things, but usually the shift is subtler—a new alertness and appreciation for the possibilities that we have left untouched in our regular liturgy. Like the tides of the sea, the variations in worship keep our services fresh and brimming with life.

Make Selections in Light of the Total Liturgy

A large part of creating an order of worship is choosing what you will use. The committee's work together has yielded an abundance of suggestions. Someone has heard a song at a summer conference which centers directly on the Scripture to be used. Another person reminds us that one of the congregation's all-time favorite hymns is a meditation on the main word of the theme we have chosen. Someone else has been working on writing a prayer which will draw together the several concerns we have discovered to be part of the main theme.

The time has come to end our dreaming and considering possibilities. Specific choices must be made. I often find it difficult to sit down to do this. Putting it off, I realize after many years, is an indirect acknowledgment that this is important work. If I were dealing with something less significant, I could easily make my choices and be done. Procrastination is for me a signal that there is a lot at stake here so I tend to postpone my decisions. But members of the worship committee expect to review the final plans soon. Sometimes that involves a meeting, but more often we simply pass around a scrap copy of the bulletin asking for any final suggestions. In either case, the *dead*line is *life*-giving. We must begin.

Several items on the list suggested by the committee have become inappropriate. These had been promising ideas in the early stages of planning. Later, however, as committee discussion developed, the theme has taken a different focus. These earlier suggestions would no longer enhance the service; so we drop them.

The formality or informality of the service may have eliminated certain styles of prayer, music, drama, or dance. This is not a once-and-for-all veto. For this particular service certain forms will not be appropriate; so we shall save them for another occasion.

A word about trust and respect among committee and staff must be included here because our effectiveness as worship planners and leaders is directly proportionate to the attention we give to the preservation of that trust. Suggestions made in committee sometimes are made "off the top of the head" during open discussion, but other times they are the "widow's mite" in spirit (Luke 21:2). If a single title or idea is all a person has, and if it is offered as representative of the contributor's very self, rejection can be painful. Yet it is impossible to incorporate all suggestions into the service we are planning. Decisions on specific inclusions must be made on the basis of many considerations. Whatever use is made of suggestions offered in committee, care must be given to the sense in which suggestions are made. Individual and group responses in committee meetings must reflect our faithful concern for each other fully as much as the worship we plan reflects our faithful concern for the spiritual growth and expression of the entire congregation.

Congregations are not inspired by services planned in an

atmosphere of dissension and political maneuvering. There is less opportunity for these things to find a toehold among us when God's Holy Spirit is understood to be present in the planning process.

We return to the list of committee suggestions. Here is a hymn which someone has suggested, referring to it as "my favorite hymn." It is a fine one all right and undoubtedly a favorite of other people in the congregation as well. But it is not related to the theme of the service. I will mention to the committee the strengths of the hymn and suggest another date we will plan to use it.

Everything else on the list looks solid. Each item has integrity; that is, it fits the service in every way. The junior choir anthem suggested by the choir director is within the range of the children's ability to sing well. They will be able to memorize it easily because the text is built of words they understand. It will be just right as a response to the Old Testament reading, and the theme and mood lead directly to the New Testament reading which follows it.

We do not have a title yet from the senior choir director for that group's anthem. He attended the planning meeting; so he has a clear understanding of the design of the service. It will be important to know the specific anthem before we can place it in the order of service. Music sung at the offertory is different from what might be sung during Communion. And there is a possibility that the choir may not present an anthem at all. Instead, they might lead the people in singing a psalm. The choir would sing the verses and the congregation a refrain. Perhaps this form will be their choice for the service. I telephone and talk it through with the director.

The prayer written by a committee member is here on the desk already. It is a fine one. It will function well to express our thanksgiving and our concerns. Amen!

But the liturgy would be well served by two more selections in which the congregation participates. Everything on the list of suggestions has been either placed or eliminated. At this moment I turn to my library, and my thought spontaneously breaks into prayer: O God, there is so much from which to choose. The shelves overflow into the closet of the study. Two filing cabinets are bulging with material eagerly collected from the music stores and publishers' catalogs. Everything is organized and cross-referenced. The newest, the accepted standards, and the most promising are within arm's reach. What will most touch the people's hearts for this occasion, Lord? What will open them to know your presence as we sing and pray?

If the selection is familiar, they will relax and sense your hand on them today as it has been the many other times they have sung this hymn. A strongly traditional hymn will help them listen to the cloud, will strengthen their sense of the church as your body, Lord. We need that as we prepare to go forth into the world to do your work.

Yet new music written through your inspiration can be so glorious, O God. It sparks us again with the sense of your Spirit. Some will grumble at the unfamiliar tune, but we will make certain it is the only new congregational music in the service and hope the disturbance will be only temporary. Perhaps the inherent strength and beauty of the music will ease the discomfort of the get-acquainted period. In fact, it is not too late to arrange to have the choir introduce this music next Sunday. Our people will know it well by the day of the service we are planning.

At last the design is complete. It is balanced and beautifully colored. Its outlines and the plan of its inner parts reflect our gifts and skills. How joyful to imagine the people's praise and prayer guided upward and supported by the tapestry we have woven. Surely this will soar all the way to heaven!

As usual, dear Lord, it has been a struggle. There are so many details to consider and balance. But, also as usual, we have felt your hand on ours as we reached for the books to consult and wrote down our ideas. Stay with us now as we continue our work. Let us never forget that your people are our care. May our efforts draw us and them ever closer to you. In Jesus' name. Amen.

Prepare Adequately

By now the service is set; theme, order, and selections are all fixed in place. But they still have to get from the page into our hearts, to be transformed from concepts into living expressions of praise. That requires adequate preparation on the part of every worship leader.

The choirs usually need the most lead time. If new music is to be sung, it must be ordered, learned by the leaders, and rehearsed by the singers. If we want to reproduce music, we will have to write for permission from the copyright owners. We might be tempted to avoid this time-consuming task if it were not for the need to maintain the integrity of our calling. Taking someone's work without permission or compensation is stealing. The finest worship service we can design will be a mockery of Christian principles and a misleading example to the congregation if copyrighted materials are printed in the program without the owner's permission.

The bulletin itself is extremely important to the worship service, for its careful layout and wording make the congregation able to participate with the minimum of attention to it. Many spoken directions can be eliminated by an effective bulletin. Type the first draft as soon as possible so that corrections and improvements may be incorporated into it. List announcements on another page, if possible, so that as much space as possible is available for the liturgy. A cramped bulletin is difficult to follow. Psychic energy drained off to figure out where we are in the service results in less attentiveness to the Spirit.

While it may not be necessary to rehearse the entire service, leaders should practice whatever is new before attempting it during worship. Walking and talking it through will uncover the unexpected in rehearsal rather than in the service. Leaders who themselves are worshipers cannot be distracted by anxiety about untidy details.

A recent experience reminded us again of the importance of gathering participants together for even a brief rehearsal. When a rehearsal first was suggested, everyone agreed the week was too busy. Besides, was it really necessary? All of us were experienced worship leaders. What sort of preparation was necessary to read the brief drama which was to be presented as the sermon? The worship committee had already spent many hours to precision tune the play for this congregation. They had elim-inated sarcasm which seemed abrasive and references that were no longer funny because of dated subject matter. Everything had been adjusted and retyped. *We all read expressively,* we thought. *What further preparation is necessary?*

A pervasive discomfort, however, lingered among us so that we finally agreed to a single rehearsal of one hour. We met in the church in the late afternoon the day before the service. Our uneasiness was well founded. Only when we stood in our care-fully worked out places, did we realize that some of our planning had been inadequate. What seemed perfect on paper proved to require something more in execution.

"When your big statement is given, you will need to step forward, or else people will be searching for the speaker rather than listening to the message."

"We need a space there; it doesn't sound like a direct quotation if it continues directly as part of the preceding statement."

"Just a few measures of musical introduction are needed there; the one written in the script takes too long and interrupts the flow of the play."

As planners, we never could have imagined how the people's appearances and speed of delivery would affect the message. We needed this rehearsal, brief though it was.

Having corrected the basic balance so that the message was clear throughout the presentation, we found ourselves gaining momentum. Now the suggestions were for polishing that which we sensed was already quite good.

"Stand up in the pulpit. Your part really functions as narrator."

"Jut out your jaw. The character will sound more arrogant that way."

We had been thoroughly convinced of the importance of this play's prophetic message, but now we were quite excited at the prospect of presenting it effectively. Our time together had primed us to summon our best potential for the service the next day.

But it is not accurate to say that everyone shared that response. One of the players called me on the telephone that evening. "I just can't go through with it," I heard at the other end of the line. "I believe in everything the play stands for, but suddenly I have realized that people could be disturbed by it, and I cannot bring myself to be a part of bringing pain to others."

Apparently the life which had developed in the text during the rehearsal had given meaning and potential for eliciting response which had not been noticed before. It was fortunate that this had occurred in rehearsal rather than in the service. One of the other readers was able to take over his part, giving the original player the time needed to step back for reflection.

The next morning when we gathered together, we discovered others whose anxiety exceeded the "butterflies" normally present before a public presentation. Here our adequate preparation took the form of prayer. Standing in a circle in the sacristy, we kept silence for a very long time. Then someone blurted out, "O God, I feel so frightened. These are your words we will read and it is your will, we believe, that they be preached. But, Lord, I am shaking. What will people say about me? Will they think I am setting myself up as perfect, as judging them? Help me, Lord. Help us."

Words now echoed around the circle of prayer:

"Help us and guide us, Lord."

"Let us speak your truth with humility."

"Help us."

Then silence and amens.

We smiled and embraced one another. Still shaking the slightest bit, we stood with confidence in the doorway, prepared in mind and spirit to enter the chancel.

Make Adjustments

The last-minute change of readers in the chancel drama was necessary, but there was no way we could have foreseen it during the planning stages. Sometimes it is more difficult to make an adjustment this late in the process. If the item is someone's favorite hymn, or if considerable effort has already been expended toward its preparation, strong reaction may occur at the mention of its possible loss. Reactions must be considered, but fear of them is no reason to avoid a necessary change.

I find it helpful to think of these adjustments as insurance against disaster. Last year's junior choir anthem for Palm Sunday was a traditional text set to bright new music. After two rehearsals, however, it was clear that even the bright new music could not succeed in establishing the text in the children's minds. Words like "Thy last and fiercest strife is nigh" had no meaning for them. No matter how many times we rehearsed each line, their faces were blank when we went back to the three which had preceded it. It was frightening to consider beginning work on a different piece with only three weeks left before Palm Sunday. Besides, we had invested two full rehearsals on the original anthem. But consideration of the disaster which was likely to occur for us all finally made me put aside the first choice. The replacement music was simpler because the time was short, but any lack of melodic brilliance was amply replaced by youthful enthusiasm in the choir's voices.

Remember, however, that it is important to avoid tinkering with the essentials of the service, particularly if the committee has carefully deliberated the choice of a certain aspect of the worship plans. Here we risk misunderstanding and weakening of trust among those who plan the liturgies.

Sometimes adding up and rechecking all the elements in the service turns out a disturbing total: there is too much unfamiliar music for the congregation to sing. When a hymn text is important and fitting and you absolutely do not want to give up the words, the metrical index may provide a means of finding a well-known tune the people can sing to the text you will be using.

First, look at the page on which the hymn is printed to discover its meter—"7.6.7.6." "Short Meter" (sometimes abbreviated S.M.), etc.

Then turn to the metrical index and locate the same meter. The text of your hymn will fit all the tunes listed in that category.

Next choose a good, old, familiar tune which matches the mood and sense of the words. Be sure to sing the text to the tune you select to make certain the poetic accents fall on the musical accents. If they do not, pick another tune from the index.

Rehearse the choir with this altered arrangement, so they can provide solid support for the congregation.

Finally, let the pastor announce in the service, "We will be using a tune different from the one printed with the words on the hymnal page." Many who do not read music may not notice the difference, but it is important pastoral care to welcome people into this new territory of worship experience and minimize confusion the first time you try it.

In fact, this is hardly a new practice. The cloud has used it for centuries! In colonial American churches, the "clerk gave out the metrical Psalms"[8] by singing the tune so that the people would know which of the many tunes was to be used with a chosen text. At no cost to a congregation, texts can be revitalized and, in some cases, made available for the first time by the sensitive substitution of another tune in the same meter.

The process also works in reverse. You may have chosen a hymn not for its words but for its tune, its melody, or its rhythm. However, the words do not match the theme of the service. In this case you can use the metrical index to discover more fitting texts in the hymnal which you can then sing to the chosen tune.

You even may wish to write some words yourself to supply the precise meaning and mood you seek. Many times we have taken the germ of an existing hymn and added verses for our congregation's specific celebration. During a service in which we were meditating on the gentleness of our Lord, we wanted to use the tune, "Fairest Lord Jesus," at the Communion time. These words were written for that occasion:

> Bread, wine, our very selves,
> Gifts you sent us from above,
> We now return with our thanks and praise.
> We hunger for your love,
> We thirst for righteousness
> And seek to serve you all our days.
>
> Heart, soul and mind and strength
> To your table these we bring.
> To you, the Christ, we give all we are.
> Your praises shall we sing,

Your ways of love shall keep,
Your truth will guide us near and far.

Faith, hope, above all, love
Give to us through wine and bread.
Then send us off to declare your grace,
Telling where we've been fed,
Sharing your life, your joy
With every nation, group, and race.

Adjustments are necessary all along the way. Our hearts and minds must be open as we continue renewing life in our congregation through worship. Receptivity to the Spirit keeps us in a state of becoming as we plan, prepare, and adjust our worship for the glory of God.

Worship God!

"I feel I can't worship except on those Sundays when I'm sitting in the pew. Most of the time I'm worrying about all the details—will the choir come in on time and will the ushers start forward when they should and will the organist remember to turn off the blower during the prayers and will . . . ?"

How often we have heard these sad words or others like them! Behind them lies something beautiful: the desire to lead the congregation in worship as effectively as possible. But they represent an approach that defeats the very hope which prompts them. Since worship is prayer, the first requirement of effective worship leadership is that the leaders themselves be in an attitude of prayer, a state of openness and communion with God whom the church has gathered to worship. That cannot happen when we are preoccupied by anxiety for how things will go. Of course, the details matter, that is why we have spent so much time on the eight steps preceding this one. Like adjusting the crossbow on a kite, tending to the details is a necessary part of our preparation, but having everything perfectly set is no guarantee we shall soar with the wind.

Leading worship is strikingly similar to playing music. I recall how my flute teacher would get me ready for a public performance. He would drill me hard, making me repeat the most difficult passages until they were flawless, refining my variations of accent and vibrato. But as the concert approached, my teacher eased back from the details. His last instructions always went something like this: "If you make a mistake, play boldly on and sing with all your heart because it is the spirit of the music that people are listening for." And it is the Spirit of the living God that people are listening, looking, and waiting for in worship. So the ushers come forward with the offering before the organist has played the introduction to the doxology or the choir stands up a little too quickly or the fire siren goes off during the sermon or a child cries in the middle of the silent prayer; yes, it would be more effective if these things did not happen and some of them can be avoided in the future through a kind and loving word, but none of these things will be as consistently destructive to worship as anxious leadership: the eyes always looking at the watch, the body tense about when to stand and sit, the voice constricted with the burden of thinking, "What comes next?"

Nothing is more helpful to worship than the example of a leader's prayerful communion with God, who has brought us together and whose everlasting mercy surely extends to those who miss their cue on Sunday because they were "Lost in wonder, love, and praise."

We suggest two ways of entering into that prayerful state. The first is the process which we have been sharing with you. Because representative members of the congregation have helped us prepare the worship and are leading many parts of the service themselves, we feel the church lifting and supporting us. The congregation is not an audience that has purchased tickets to judge our virtuosity but a community of pilgrims joining with us on a journey to a single goal: the source of our birth and being, the eternal spring of faith, hope, and love. We travel together, depending on one another's company and rejoicing in everyone's gifts and contributions.

Yet before the entire congregation sets off on the journey together, before the first note of the prelude sounds, there is one final preparation: gathering all the leaders together for prayer. Now is not the moment to fret about details. Now is the moment to pray for the Holy Spirit without whose presence all of our preparations will not matter.

I can still remember as a child our pastor praying with our youth choir just before we processed into the service—not that I was paying close attention. As the Reverend Highberger began, I was usually looking across the room at Janet, who liked me a lot, or I was poking Bruce Logan in the ribs if he was not poking me first. But somewhere in the middle of the minister's prayer I would pull my hand away from Bruce and take my eyes off Janet and bow my head. I was still the same rambunctious child that I had been seconds before, but it had dawned on me in that primitive, simple way these things dawn on children: we're doing this for God.

Here then are two ways to lead worship from an attitude of prayer:

Prepare thoroughly before the day of worship.

Pray fervently at the hour of worship.

Then let the music sound and the praise begin! Let the congregation rise to its feet and let everyone sing. Everyone! The skeptic in the floppy hat, the legalist, the reticent believer, and the devoted disciple. Let us all join in singing a glad and faithful song. We're doing this for God! And as those words flame in our souls, we detect the first stirrings of a breeze which swells in stronger gusts of prayers and praise until the whole church is soaring, soaring with the wind!

Evaluate

Click.

6:58

Another day

—ohhh, a Monday.

I walk over to the TV.

The earth appears above the moon.

6:59

I rub the sleep from my eyes and listen to the echoes of indecipherable dreams.

7:00

TODAY

More victims.

I am "perplexed, but not driven to despair" (2 Corinthians 4:8*b*).

Why?

Because yesterday we soared with the wind. I have no illusion of swift and easy salvation. But I have the strength to act, to attend the meeting, to write the letter, to make the phone call, to give the money, to stand for mercy and for justice. Not because I am good or noble because I am not. But because we were lifted by the Spirit yesterday in church. Yes, there were some things we needed to improve, and we will be discussing them in our worship committee. We will be reviewing in love all that went well and all that required more attention. We will not dismiss anyone's reaction, negative or positive, but we will try to understand what the worship was like for the congregation.

Did we define the situation accurately?

Did we probe the treasures of Scripture and cloud effectively?

Did we identify the theme clearly?

Was the style of the service appropriate?

Did the order of worship embody the theme?

Were the selections in keeping with the total liturgy?

Had we prepared adequately?

Were our adjustments on target?

Above all, did we move beyond these details into a state of prayer in which we worshiped God with all our heart and all our soul and all our mind and all our strength?

Then having evaluated what happened, we will begin the process again, thankful for all that has been revealed through our worship and filled with wonder at "the depth of the riches and wisdom and knowledge of God!" (Romans 11:33).

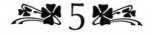

5

Put Your Feet Back on Earth

Dealing with Resistance

There is a sacred chamber in the heart where we store the meanings of our lives. The order of worship and the arrangement of the nave give material expression to that interior reality. Change something on the outside and you may disturb something on the inside. Alterations to worship may shake the sanctuary of the heart so that people bolt the door and resist with all the strength they possess.

"We never tried that before. It won't work here."

Resistance to change often evokes one of two disastrous reactions: acquiescence or rebellion. The first fills us with the toxic wastes of resentment which corrode our souls and spirit. The second snaps the link of pastoral care between those who resist and the church leadership. There is, however, another response: to view resistance as an opportunity to help the congregation grow in the love and knowledge of God. "When the people say no, ministry may have been reached."[1]

Worship reform requires not only that we listen to the cloud and soar with the wind but also that we put our feet back on earth and deal with the resistance to change. How we do that varies according to the congregation's reactions. Our first step is to identify why people are resisting:

Is it because the change threatens a world of private meaning?

Is it because someone thinks, "We don't have what it takes to do that"?

Is it a misperception of how other members of the congregation will react?

Is it a concern to preserve that which the church holds sacred?

There may be other complex factors below the surface, but these four questions can help you locate the primary source of resistance. We have ordered them to move from the personal to the most corporate. Whether you are dealing with an individual problem or a reaction from a larger portion of the congregation makes a difference in how you address the resistance.

A Threatened World of Private Meaning

Someone comes out of a service furious that you have put new words to a beloved hymn tune. The hurt in the voice and the eyes indicates that something more is going on than a mere difference of taste. That change must have turned the sacred chamber of this person's heart upside down and cracked some treasured meaning. Other people come out the door and say, "I like the new verses to the old hymn."

What do you do?

You have no desire to hurt anyone. Just the opposite: you hope that worship will be an occasion of healing and joy. You are tempted to acquiesce. You can still hear the pleading and resentment in the voice, "Why did you ever change the words to my favorite hymn?" Imagine what the reaction will be from that person if you try the new words of the hymn a second time! So you make your decision: never again.

But then you remember the enthusiasm with which many people sang. An engineer, the high school physics teacher, and a teenager all mentioned how they liked the words about the galaxies and about distant solar systems because they brought the scientific perspective into the service. And that was exactly one of the things you had talked about in the worship committee:

the need, as one parent had put it, "to let our children know the church is not just a religious museum." Thinking on all of these positive benefits, you are now tempted to rebel completely against the critic; we will sing the hymn again next Sunday.

Then the image of the hurt eyes and the sound of the resentful voice at the door return to your mind, and you flip back to your original decision: never again.

Next Sunday.

Never again.

Next Sunday.

Never again.

Next Sunday.

Never again.

Your struggle indicates the need for a more sophisticated response than acquiescence or rebellion. So you begin to analyze the situation, noting that the resistance is coming from one individual. There may be other people who were not thrilled with the hymn, but every indication is that it was well received by most members, and they want to sing it again. You decide to go to the individual, not to accuse nor to beat into submission but to understand what is going on in that person's soul that such resentment could be awakened by a seemingly simple change.

The pastor on whose story this case is based found out the hymn was a "favorite" because it had been sung at the funeral of the individual's mother. "Whenever we sing it, I remember Mom and I think of her being with God now. When you changed the words, it seemed like you were taking away my comfort." The pastor reports that there followed a long conversation which touched on childhood memories, unhealed wounds, and where people go when they die. Before the pastor left, they also discussed how other church members had responded positively to the hymn. The grieving individual was now able to climb beyond the walls of a private world of meaning to consider the larger universe of truth. It would be "okay" to sing the new verses again.

All of this came out of changing the words to a hymn *and* out of a pastor's refusal to get hooked into the simple patterns of acquiescence or rebellion. An act of worship reformation thus became an occasion of pastoral care. Not only had the change reached the engineer, the physicist, and the high school student and helped them to worship, but also through the unforeseen workings of the Spirit it brought healing and growth to a soul in pain.

If you begin to reform your worship, you will inevitably encounter situations like this one. And it will not always be the pastor who will have to follow up on the negative reaction. Sometimes the worship committee will need to serve as leaven in the lump, as people who listen sensitively to the resistance of individuals and help relate the world of private meaning to the larger universe of the church's understanding. Getting ready for this kind of ministry should be part of your worship preparation. It may seem like a large task. It is! But then it represents nothing more than the command of the New Testament that we live together in love. Worship reform thus leads us far beyond the particulars of liturgical change into the heart of the community's life. If we are not prepared for this, then it would be kinder and more honest of us "not to rock the boat" and to leave things as they are. But what possibilities we shall be losing!

We Don't Have What It Takes to Do That

"Our congregation is not like the ones you have described," we often hear. "There isn't even a glimmer of imagination here. People think the best service is whatever is most like last week's and the week before. We are good people, but we just don't have what it takes to rejuvenate our worship."

Reading about the worship of other communities inevitably calls forth comparisons. It is difficult to imagine achieving similar results without a person like the story's central character. "Sure we could do the same if only So and So didn't sabotage every suggestion and talk against it to others in the congregation."

The stories in this book are true. The people are real. What continues to reassure us is that, even among congregations who do achieve much progress in revitalizing worship, there is no personality profile for leadership or size of committee or staff able to be identified as a necessary component of that progress.

Where faith is present and there is determination to work out God's will and community continues, people can be agents for restoration of life and health to the worshiping congregation.

There are good reasons to be discouraged sometimes. Every church has its limitations. But far too frequently we cut off the possibilities for change with unfounded projections of inadequacy. "We don't have what it takes to do that here" is an assumption that should always be questioned. Worship renewal cannot take root where this statement is allowed to become a self-fulfilling prophecy.

Some years ago, our choir was invited to lead the Sunday morning worship in a small church about thirty miles away from ours. Our own pastor was willing to have us go for one Sunday. In fact, he had suggested that our choir's presence might spark the congregation's interest in forming a choir of their own. Our pastor had been serving on an advisory committee for assisting smaller churches in the area. He had described the other pastor's considerable knowledge and ardent love of church music and how earnestly he had expressed his wish to have a choir develop in his congregation. The church had an organ and a capable musician to play it for the services, but a choir had not functioned in the parish for years.

The brisk and sunny Sunday morning gave us a sense of adventure as we filled the cars with "singers-to-go." We would present one anthem from our repertoire and lead the people in the worship service music and hymns. The small church resounded with the voices of the people singing, and we were touched by their appreciative faces and the thankfulness they expressed to us at the coffee hour which followed the service.

"Would you like to establish a choir in your congregation?" I asked one person during our conversation.

"Oh, we would love to have a choir, but we are not allowed," she said.

"Who could prevent your having a choir if you could organize some singers?" I asked in amazement.

"We have tried each fall for the past three years to establish a group," she went on. "We rehearse for about two months, but the minister says we cannot sing in church until we sound good enough; and since we are small, we really don't sound as good as the city choirs, so he never thinks we are good enough and people stop coming to rehearsal and every year the effort flops. We just don't have what it takes to have music leadership here."

When most of the parishioners had gone home, the minister invited me into his study. He seemed genuinely appreciative that our people had made the hour's drive to be with the congregation. But when we talked about developing a choir program in the church, he said he was even more convinced now that there could never be such a thing in a congregation of that size. "God requires the very best," he began, "and people must be reminded of that at all times. Our denomination has a fine tradition of choral music which must be honored and perpetuated. How can three people sing four-part music? I simply cannot allow a choir in the service until it measures up to what I know is expected of a church of this denomination."

He thought the idea of a choir functioning as leadership for the congregation's singing was a "waste of time." There was no need, in his opinion, for a choir to assist in introducing new music to the congregation because "we don't do any new music." I told him something of the modest beginnings of our own choir and how, from time to time, illness and business trips took people away from rehearsals, causing us to sing three-part, two-part, and even unison pieces sometimes. But I had the distinct impression that the pastor heard this as narrative rather than as a working principle.

My heart was heavy as I drove through the beautiful countryside toward home. That church did have what it takes to have a choir, not a choir to fill a cathedral with music but a choir that would sound just right in their small and lovely building. The minister's overinflated expectation was blinding him to what the possibilities were, and we have seen this happen again and again. A church wants to try a dramatic sermon, but someone says, "We don't have what it takes to do that," meaning "We don't have what it takes to build a set and put on a Broadway production." And the person is right. But who is talking about a Broadway production? This is going to be worship drawing on the resources we do have. Keep it simple. Maybe a single prop or reading in the round or an engaging picture on the bulletin cover is all it will take to grip the imagination of the congregation in a powerful way.

Every time someone says, "We don't have what it takes to do *that*," ask, "What's your definition of *that*?" Does *that* mean Beethoven's *Missa Solemnis* or a hymn in two parts? Does *that* mean a televised revival in a stadium of thousands or a ritual of rededication done in a style to which your congregation can respond? Does *that* mean a dance by the New York City Ballet or a graceful procession of persons carrying the Bible down the aisle to symbolize the entrance of God's Word into the midst of our lives?

In part we are all victims of the electronic media. We daily hear the greatest performers on records, cassettes, radio, and television, and they become the unrealistic standard of our worship. Naturally, we want our services to go as well as possible, but the way to achieve that is not to saddle ourselves with impossible expectations. New possibilities for worship are all around us. Like the figures hidden in the line drawings of a child's puzzle book, they are visible yet concealed by the shapes which surround them and the expectations of the viewer. It requires an unprejudiced and probing eye to discern them. Imagine what it would be like if that small country church did organize a choir. Maybe the skeptic in the floppy hat would show up for rehearsals. I have known many skeptics who have sung their way to faith. Or imagine what would happen if the worship committee decided to have some regular rite of rededication. Who knows what pledge of loyalty might spring from the heart of the reticent disciple? Or imagine your church not paralyzed by the words "We don't have what it takes to do that here," but instead trying to. . . .

We will let you complete that last sentence for yourselves. You are the only ones who can. That is our point: neither we nor anyone else has a prepackaged program that will fit your worship needs. Your praise of God must arise from your congregation's life together. Look around your community with eyes unburdened by projections of inadequacy and the words of our Lord will become true for you: "'But blessed are your eyes, for they see, and your ears, for they hear'" (Matthew 13:16). And blessed is your worship because you have taken the gifts that were given you and used them for the glory of God.

Misperceptions of How Others Will React

Sometimes we project our fears not onto the task but onto other people. We hold an image in our heads of who they are and how they will react. This image is more real to us than the actuality of their character, and it controls the expression of our desires and hopes.

"It'll never work in our church. *They* wouldn't like it."

Who are these "they"? Are they others as they truly are or as we imagine them to be? In a course on worship renewal involving participants from twenty-five churches, it became apparent that this "they" was the projected image which ministers and lay people cast upon one another. The sponsoring group had scheduled the program so that we met with the laity on Sunday afternoons and the clergy the following Monday. During our third meeting, when we discussed many of the ideas contained in our chapter "Soar with the Wind," the lay leaders indicated that they were thrilled at the possibilities for reforming their worship but knew "It'll never work in our church. *They* wouldn't like it."

"Who are 'they'?" we asked.

"The ministers!" several voices announced in a tone indicating they considered it a self-evident truth that clergy are opposed to reforming worship.

The next day we presented the same material to the clergy. Again there was excitement about the new possibilities for Sunday morning until someone indicated he did not believe any of it would work. When asked why, several ministers explained, "The congregation won't accept it." This charge was made in the same self-evident tone that the lay people had used the day before!

Each side was excited about revitalizing worship and each saw the other as opposed. A situation like this sometimes tends to be more complex than it first seems. It may be that neither party favors change; yet neither wants to appear opposed. So each blames the other. In this case, however, it was simpler than that. Both sides wanted to reform their worship; that was apparent from the time commitment they made to the course and their enthusiastic participation. People do not fake that kind of thing. When the lay people and ministers discovered what each had said of the other, they smiled, even laughed at themselves. In the following months many of them came to the course filled with stories of things they had tried together, "things we thought we could never do." What had appeared as insurmountable resistance proved to be little more than unwarranted projections of how others would react.

The fact that we were outsiders and therefore viewed as neutral helped us fill the role of mediators between the two parties. Looking back at the entire course, we believe that the most valuable thing we did was to relieve clergy and laity of their misperceptions of each other.

Perhaps your church could use someone from the outside to help you move beyond mistaken projections of what "they"— whoever "they" may be—think and feel. Yet even without an intermediary present, you can facilitate healthy change in your church's worship by never assuming that you know what "they" will or will not allow. Disciplining your deliberations in this way is taking seriously the wonder and complexity of the human soul and building a community of trust.

Preserving What Is Sacred

Marion Barrett "considered the interim prayer book an abomination" because it differed from the act of worship she had always known (page 10). The adults in my home church frowned at the Sunday school for singing music that was not part of the congregation's tradition (page 58). The opponents of the Tenebrae service feared it would diminish the meaning of Maundy Thursday (page 98). In each situation people resisted a change in the familiar order because they were determined to preserve what they thought was holy. But in doing so, they reduced the sacred to a fixed form.

Wise worship leadership in cases like these proceeds by affirming what is healthy in the resistance without acquiescing to liturgical idolatry. We honor the intention but do not give in to the distortion. That is exactly what the worship committee of the church trying its first Tenebrae service did. They agreed with the opponents about the need to maintain the sacredness of Maundy Thursday, and they led a service which, though different, was still faithful to that goal. The resistance continued until people participated in the service. Rational argument could never have taken the congregation over that final step into enthusiastic acceptance. It was the experience of worship, the encounter with Christ at his candlelit table, which convinced them and which carried them into a more comprehensive vision of the sacred.

Helping a church to avoid the idolatry of form is a vital role for any congregation's leadership. Nathan, the prophet, fills this function with King David. David is eager to build God a house, to set God up in a temple as fine as his palace. Though David's motivation may be noble and devout, God sees how the action is filled with possibilities for idolatry and sends Nathan to say to the king, "'Are you the one to build me a house to live in? I have not lived in a house since the day I brought up the people of Israel from Egypt to this day, but I have been moving about in a tent and a tabernacle'" (2 Samuel 7:5b–6). So even before the first spade of earth is turned and the cornerstone laid, there is tension between a templing people and a tenting God. God does not require a temple; we do. Out of love God accedes to our need for visible symbols. Then we turn it all around and hold as eternally sacred what only points to God. We forget that God alone is holy.

King Solomon also sees the danger of such distortion. He dedicates the temple with a prayer which reminds us how much greater God is than any form or structure we create. "'But will God indeed dwell on the earth? Even heaven and the highest heaven cannot contain you, much less this house that I have built!'" (1 Kings 8:27). And how much less can any one denomination or tradition or style of music or way of praying contain God!

Again and again the wisdom of Nathan's prophecy and Solomon's prayer is lost as we attempt to confine the tenting God to the temple, to the structures of worship which we have always known. Of course, it is necessary to have some dependable pattern for our worship—we have stressed that in our chapter "Soar with the Wind"—but equally necessary is a spiritual vigilance against the idolatry of form. It is possible to use worship not to praise God but to escape God. We cling to what we know in order to avoid the sovereignty of our uncontainable Lord. Instead of using the symbols of faith to be drawn into an expanding awareness of God, we use them to fix God in place, to keep the illusion that we are in control. Liturgical form itself is not the problem but rather the posture of the soul, the attitude of the heart. Working through this resistance involves more than debating the details of worship. We must be prepared to ask ourselves as well as others:

Are we preserving what is sacred?

or

Are we avoiding the Holy God whom "heaven and highest heaven cannot contain"?

The tone in which we raise the question is crucial. Arrogance is never appropriate, as if we alone possessed the sacred truth and never ourselves resisted the working of the Spirit. Each of us, like King David, is susceptible to the illusion that heaven depends on the house, the form, the liturgy we would build for God. If we acknowledge this, if we are in touch with our own resistance to altering what we consider holy, then there will be no haughtiness in our voice and no condescension in our eyes when we deal with others who are upset because the service is changed. The ultimate way, then, of learning how to deal with resistance is to open that chamber of the heart where we store the meanings of our lives and confess to God our own idolatries:

> King David, Lord, we think was right
> To want a house for you.
> A tent seems flimsy, small and light—
> To state the monarch's view.

> For One who made us flesh and bone
> Who orders time and space,

It seems we ought to build with stone
A rich and regal place.

We'll give our best of gold and art.
We'll sing, we'll dance, we'll pray.
We only ask you play your part
And let us have our way:

No moving out beyond the nave,
No bringing in what's new,
Just give our souls the peace they crave
And heal our bodies too.

The temple air grows stale and dead.
Our praise begins to tire.
The forms on which we once were fed
Now lack your wind and fire.

Oh, yet we fear to change a thing
"It's what God wants," we say.
No wonder, then, you told the king
His plans to put away.

You knew what idols we would mold,
Would bless with your own name,
As if from heaven we were told
To keep our prayers the same.

Let Nathan's words again resound,
"Would you build God a home?
God won't be caught or closed or bound.
God wants to move and roam."

Grant now to us a tenting soul,
Not tied to wood or stone,
But fixed forever on this goal:
The praise of you alone.[2]

❧ 6 ❧

Become Instruments in God's Hands

Dancing for the Lord

When Mikail Baryshnikov joined the New York City Ballet, he said he wanted to be under the direction of the company's world-renowned choreographer, George Balanchine, because: "'I would love to be the instrument in his wonderful hands.'"[1] Despite his dazzling technique, Baryshnikov realized that the greatest talent wears thin if it is not at the service of some larger pattern of meaning and movement.

When we worship, we seek to become instruments in God's wonderful hands by joining a pattern of meaning and movement greater than our individual lives. Every service is a "dance." If you doubt the metaphor, reflect on a time when you attended worship in a tradition far different from your own. Remember how anxious you were to know when to stand or sit or bow. All worship services involved organized movement, and organized movement is dance. The first time you worshiped in that new setting, you had not yet learned the "steps." You were probably less attentive to the Spirit and more occupied in keeping your place in the service and doing things right. This is one of the main reasons why churches follow regular patterns of ritual, not in order to shackle the community's life to a single form but in order to free people to "dance" with grace before the presence of God. If every Sunday the entire congregation had to learn a new pattern, they would be utterly exhausted and never get to throw themselves with abandon into the praise of God.

And yet if they did only the same "dance" over and over, their worship would become stale. Baryshnikov acknowledged that he needed to learn new roles in order to "'develop things that I don't have yet.'"[2] Likewise, congregations need to expand their repertory of worship in order to develop aspects of faith and praise they do not yet have.

Worship, like all dances, requires that we practice the steps until the mechanics become second nature and we can give ourselves to the beat and flow of the music. Whether our church's "dance" is new or old, the aim is still the same: to be instruments in God's wonderful hands.

Earlier in this book we suggested that you walk through a typical worship service to raise your awareness of what people are experiencing from different positions inside the church. We tried to become sensitive to how things appear and sound, whether the physical arrangement of space—the height of the pulpit, the position of the Lord's table, the location of the choir— were aiding or detracting from the service (see pages 29ff.). Now we want to focus on how we as worship leaders stand, gesture, and move, in short how we "dance" for God.

Standing and Moving with Grace

Consider a simple thing like standing. It is not as simple as you may think. People draw important messages by looking at us, particularly in moments of stress or surprise, when the rehearsed facade is suspended. It is not too much to say that the state of our souls, which is critical to our effectiveness as worship leaders, is written all over us. If we feel depressed, our neck and shoulders tend to slouch and our eyes tilt downward, avoiding contact with others. A worship leader who stands in such a posture and announces, "In Jesus Christ we are forgiven," may do more harm than good because the body will suggest that the words are bogus. The Bible frequently refers to sin as a burden, and the lifting of this burden sets people free to stand tall and walk boldly forward. Jesus announces to the paralytic lowered through the roof by his friends, "'Son, your sins are forgiven.'" Then he commands, "'I say to you, stand up, take your mat and go to your home.' And he stood up, and immediately took the mat and went out before all of them; so that they were all amazed and glorified God, saying, 'We have never seen anything like this!'" (Mark 2:5b and 11-12). The praise of God springs spontaneously from people who *see* the effect of God's forgiveness. Word and action form an integrated witness to the power of God's pardon.

When we stand to declare God's mercy, the congregation needs to see as well as hear the reality. Word and action must be as integrated in our services as they are in the Scriptures. Thus, if we are going to lead the congregation in a unison prayer of confession followed by a declaration of forgiveness, we prepare not only by reading through the words but also by getting in touch with the bodily reality of sin's burden and release. If I am going to be standing while reading the prayer in the service, I stand while I practice it. The weight of my sin feels different when I am on my feet than when I sink back in my easy chair. I pause after each confession in the prayer and take time to examine what it means personally for me. I sense the burden of all that I have been and not been. I can feel a growing weight that tugs me down, as if I had my canvas knapsack on my back and it were being filled with bricks. This is more than a rehearsal. This is an encounter between myself as I really am and God, a prelude to leading the congregation into a similar encounter in the worship service.

Then I say aloud the declaration of pardon: "In the name of Jesus Christ you are forgiven. If anyone is in Christ, that person is a new creation." I stop to realize that these words which I shall be speaking to the congregation are for me as well as for them. The words are not just a line in a script. They are the sword of grace cutting the weight from my back.

I feel it dropping away.

I stretch.

I stand tall.

I stand firm, glad, and light, lifted up by the freedom which Christ has given me. I am being shaped into an instrument of mercy by God's own hands. I am learning the "choreography" of confession and pardon so I can lead the entire congregation in the new creation dance.

Of course, that is not the only "dance" to be offered in the service. If you look carefully through your order of worship, you may be surprised at the number of movements which go on in your service: the procession of the choir; the standing, sitting, and bowing of the congregation; the movement of worship leaders from pulpit to table to congregation; the bringing forward of the offering; the gestures of the music director when conducting the choir or teaching the congregation a new hymn. Because we are so oriented toward the importance of the printed and spoken word, we often ignore the significance of these bodily postures and movements. Yet the simplest shifts in how we stand and walk can influence the entire spirit of a service. When choirs sing with conviction, the joyful difference in sound is clearly apparent. And when their faces and bodies reflect the same conviction, the effect on others is sometimes electrifying.

One week with some friends we visited a church in which the choir knew the opening hymn so well that when they walked in they held their heads high and looked radiantly toward the large cross that dominated the front of the church. Their voices rang out clearly because the sound was not getting strangled in throats that were bent over to look at the page in their hands. It was as if the music were pouring down from the cross into the choir and then being returned with adoration to the redemptive source from which it had first flowed. At first I thought maybe this was only my own perception, but after the service several friends mentioned it before I had said a word. We found that the effect had been basically the same on all of us: we joined in that first hymn filled with a sense of the ebullient power of God.

Several weeks later we visited another church of approximately the same size and physical layout, including a central cross up front. The choir was as large as the one weeks before;

but when it started down the aisle, the sound was smaller and more constricted. I looked to my side and saw every head staring straight down into the hymnbook, as if the only reality were the printed page and the choir members were deciphering from it some obscure message. Nothing in their posture indicated a relationship between the cross and the hymn. That opening "dance" said worship is drudgery.

What makes the story sadder is that the congregation had a strong faith in God. It became clear during the coffee hour and adult education class that these people knew Christ and cared about one another and about the world, although several said individually, "I wish we had a little more life; something's missing in our service."

The minister evidently sensed that same need himself. At the conclusion of the processional hymn he announced, "We are here to be glad and joyful in the Lord." But his words were ineffectual because they were never embodied in the postures and movements of the service. The "something missing" which people intuited without identifying was the dissonance between the verbalized message and the enacted truth.

That congregation needed to learn how to embody its praise as well as speak and sing it. This does not mean making people feel awkward by compelling them to move in ways that seem stagy or alien. Nor does it necessarily require them to develop a liturgical dance group. That can be a marvelous resource for a church, but it sometimes ends up isolating graceful movement in a few trained individuals while ignoring the rest of the congregation. The first need is for the worship leaders to become aware of their movements and postures and to consider their symbolic and emotional effect upon the congregation.

For example, choir members at the beginning of the rehearsal season could walk through a service reflecting on the meaning of each action they do and how it encourages or discourages the congregation's praise. Many churches in the past have deliberately put safely out of sight faces and bodies which have precious potential for ministry. The organ console and the one operating it often are swathed in luxurious drapes of velvet or brocade. Sometimes choir and organ are positioned behind a

permanent wall of masonry. We must ask, What benefit to congregation or musicians is derived from this separation? What
possibilities for genuine "group" singing could be realized if the
most gifted singers, the choir, were part of the larger community
through eye contact and/or different physical placement?

Some churches which have come to understand the value of
learning new music on a regular basis have experimented with
brief teaching periods just prior to the service or during the
liturgy, as it seems appropriate. The church's musician leaves
the organ console to stand in full view of the people for a few
moments of introduction and teaching of new congregational
music. At these times the simple indication of high and low
pitches by the leader's moving hand is of great assistance to
people of all ages who are trying to grasp the melodic patterns
of a new hymn or response. Many musicians have learned to
play the guitar and other instruments which allow them to lead
songs with their own voices and to have eye contact with the
people with whom they are joined together in singing praise.

All of these are ways to integrate gestures, movement, music,
and words so that sight and sound together invite the congregation to join the "dance" of worship.

Giving Body Back to Soul

One year we brought a professional dancer, Garth Fagan, to
our worshiping community.[3] Before he taught us a single step,
he asked us to go through the motions of our services: walking,
standing, holding a book, bowing in prayer. Sometimes he asked
us to move in a way that expressed a particular conviction about
God: "You believe God loves you and accepts you and you don't
have anything to fear. Knowing that, walk up to the front of the
church to lead a prayer or read the Bible." The wonder of what
Garth Fagan did was that he helped us to experience in our
bodies the truth of the gospel. God's love was not just an idea
that rearranged the molecules in our craniums, but it was a
power that animated us to move gracefully and boldly. Perhaps
best of all, the movements flowed naturally out of us, out of the
faith which we had but which we had never fully expressed
through our bodies.

In effect, Garth Fagan was helping us to respond to the apostle Paul's exhortation: "I appeal to you therefore, brothers and sisters, by the mercies of God, to present your bodies as a living sacrifice, holy and acceptable to God, which is your spiritual worship" (Romans 12:1). Note the word "bodies," *somata* in Greek. Our English word "somatic"—meaning "bodily"— comes from this term. The New English Bible uses the phrase "your very selves" instead of "bodies." But for Paul there is no separation between the body and the self. Our bodies *are* our very selves. We still preserve this corporeal understanding of our identity in phrases such as "Put your body on the line" and "Actions speak louder than words." That is exactly what Garth Fagan was helping us to do, to put our bodies on the line for God, to praise the Lord with actions as well as words, "to present [our] bodies as a living sacrifice."

Reclaiming the body in worship is a way of being more faithful to God our Creator who made us flesh and bone as well as head and heart. It is a way of bringing the totality of who we are to God, all of us for all of God.

Such a holistic approach can be threatening to people who feel comfortable with words but anxious about engaging their bodies in worship. It sometimes has seemed our Christian duty to resist with all the strength of our conviction the urge to move or sway in church. We sense the danger of excess in any pleasure we experience, and it is by no means an imaginary temptation. The early church experienced and legislated against the destructive possibilities of the spontaneous expression of faith during public worship. We have seen in the chapter "Listen to the Cloud" how the history of the church forms a roller-coaster pattern—now encouraging, now discouraging the people's full expression of faith. In its soaring moments, the gathered church has known the Spirit and has become leaven for its continuing generation among us. The historical dips have taken us to churches full of silent congregations, who listen while others speak and sing their praise to God.

Helping churches to "dance" means more than introducing another form of art into the service. It involves acknowledging how most of our communities have conditioned us to control the foot that would be tempted to tap, to subdue the body that might tend to sway as we sing. Yet despite what our heads tell us, we know in our bones that music leads inevitably to dancing. By its nature music's rhythm and melody call us to join all of ourselves in its movements. How glorious the moments when we have been among people who understand the Spirit to be present in such natural movements!

Our black brothers and sisters have allowed us a glimpse of a community free to give bodily expression to their sense of God's presence in worship. People who have grown up in churches which reflect a different heritage are frequently puzzled at what may be interpreted as an apparent lack of order. But moving, swaying, and clapping are a different kind of order, a different kind of "dance."

With God's creation as our model, we all strive for order. But we also recognize that there is a splendid variety within the universe, and we have been granted freedom to respond to the Spirit in many ways. How could we imagine that "order" always means "being still" or that "prayerful" always means "silent and meek"? The ancient preacher of Ecclesiastes tells us there is "a time to keep silence, and a time to speak" (Ecclesiastes 3:7b), and we are extending his insight to say that there is in our worship a time to be still and a time to sway and move. Is your church enjoying a full range of responses to the Spirit?

Uncoiling the Somatic Dimensions of Language

In developing a congregation's ability to "dance," we never attack their highly developed use of language in sermons, prayers, songs, and statements of faith. That is a gift to celebrate and to build on! People can learn how to "dance" more freely for God by uncoiling the somatic dimensions of the truth which they already know verbally and intellectually. For example, the "dance" of confession and pardon which we outlined earlier was suggested to us by a famous scene from John Bunyan's *The Pilgrim's Progress*. Bunyan's spiritual classic represents the highly verbal Protestant tradition at its most vivid, drawing pictures in the imagination with graphic language:

Now I saw in my dream that the highway up which Christian

was to go was fenced on either side with a wall, and that wall was called Salvation. Up this way, therefore, did burdened Christian run, but not without great difficulty, because of the load on his back.

He ran thus till he came at a place somewhat ascending, and upon that place stood a Cross, and a little below, in the bottom, a sepulchre. So I saw in my dream that just as Christian came up with the Cross his burden loosed from off his shoulders and fell from off his back and began to tumble, and so continued to do, till it came to the mouth of the sepulchre, where it fell in, and I saw it no more.

Then was Christian glad and lightsome, and said, with a merry heart, "He hath given me rest by His sorrow and life by His death."[4]

Feeling the heaviness of sin and the lightness of mercy in our bodies is not something that we do in opposition to words. Rather, our posture is the material expression of the same reality to which Bunyan's words point: the buoyancy of grace.

Sensitive attention to what our words mean for the way we stand and move will over time help most congregations become more comfortable in expressing themselves through their bodies. As this happens, you may want to expand the range of ways in which you invite people to "dance" in the service. Sometimes it may be best to introduce new movement at a retreat or during a class where people are more ready to experiment.

Here is an exercise we led at a workshop. We used a single posture to help people step into the gospel lesson of the woman bent over double, Luke 13:10-17,[5] and to act out the physical dimensions of the story. We asked everyone to stand and to bend over from the waist until his or her torso was nearly parallel to the ground, and we gave them time to act out in their own way each line that describes a motion:

I'd lie in bed if lying still I'd sleep.
But bodies need to turn or they grow sore,
And being bent, just turning is a chore.
Though nights are long, my rest is never deep.

I rise while others walk the world of dreams,
And down my angled back I pull a robe,
Then pace the floor until the cock has crowed

And morning light pours in my room in streams.

I haul a pitcher to the village well.
A broken crane that barely hoists its load,
I know each dip and hole that dents the road
And where the frost has made the cobbles swell.

A stranger says today when I am done:
"Look up! The mountain wears a dazzling crown."
But doubled over, I keep looking down
In wave-webbed water searching for the sun.

Arriving home, I hear some skylarks sing.
I guess they're skipping through the air to play.
A friend once drew their course of flight in clay.
"It's like they're climbing stairs to heaven's king.

"Imagine angels bounding up the sky.
They trace in blue the pattern at your feet."
But all I picture listening in the street
Are lines in dirt beneath my earthbound eye.

The sabbath falls. I hear a man and child.
"It's time you went to bed. Don't make me scold."
"If God is resting, who is throwing gold?"
"Come in, come in—," the father's voice turns mild.

I go to prayers before the others do
And take a place where I can rest and lean.
I'm nodding off. I hope I won't be seen . . .
"Wake up, wake up! The rabbi's calling you."

"What? Who?" They steer me toward the teacher's hand.
His words surround me—buoyant, soothing, cool.
I feel I'm wading through a healing pool.
His hand unfolds my frame. I stand. I stand!

No sun crowned peak, no skylark's upward track,
No gold that's scattered in the sky by night
Shall match my praise in breadth or depth or height:
To God alone I'll freely bend my back.[6]

By the time we got to the next to the last verse, our backs

were aching. Our bodies were yearning to be unbent. When we all stood straight, we felt in our bones the release and the joy of how Christ lifts up the bent. We followed this "dance" with a hymn whose refrain is a series of exultant alleluias. As we came to the refrain for the last time, we spontaneously put down our hymnals, stretched our hands above our heads, and arched backwards. One participant observed afterwards: "I could not believe that I was doing that. I'm usually so embarrassed just at the thought of worshiping like that. But after we did the story, it seemed perfectly natural. I wanted to stretch up for God." Being in the informal atmosphere of the conference helped free the woman. But we need to study her reaction for what it reveals about helping people over the initial awkwardness they feel in using their bodies in worship. Because the movement unfolded out of the Gospel story, it seemed "perfectly natural." The action drew on the woman's facility with words and thereby made her secure as she tried something new. This is a pattern which reduces people's sense of threat and frees them to engage more of who they are in the worship of God.

Another participant told that she had recently recovered from a back problem which had made it impossible for her to look up for several weeks. "But I never connected my healing to God until I bent over and then straightened up in the service." Our "dance" through the text had done what mere words could not. Yet notice how plain that dance was. There were only two major "steps"—standing bent and standing straight. From those actions deep insights flowed. Some people remembered how Christ had personally straightened them while others thought of Christ lifting the burdens of injustice and war so that the oppressed could stand up. Our ritual "dance" had helped people to identify where Christ is moving in the world and is inviting them to join the "dance" of love, faith, justice, and peace. And that, of course, is our final goal: to use all of ourselves in worship so that in all times and all places we may be instruments in God's wonderful hands.

7

The Kingdom
Not Yet Come
But on Its Way

Understanding Our Roles in Worship

This book began with people and it ends with people. We opened by recounting the words of a pastor—"I want to be more open to glory, and I want that for my people when we gather to worship"—and the last chapter included the responses of conference participants who "danced" through the story of the woman bent double. Throughout the book clergy and laity from every kind of church have appeared, witnesses to the joy and struggle of maintaining the worship life of a congregation. It is not incidental that we have drawn upon the experience of all these people. We have been eager to embody in our writing the principles that we are describing. And central to everything that we have presented is our belief that worship is the responsibility of the entire church. We know this to be true from our own work. Our creativity would wither without the stimulus provided by the communities of faith we serve.

We have written from our experience, often having to put the manuscript down in order to practice the organ or plan a service or discuss with sponsors the shape and content of a worship conference. Thus the book grows out of the process it is describing, a process which reveals that the Spirit is not something we have locked up and can release into congregations needing new life. Instead, the Spirit is present in and among all of God's people. To call on the Spirit in worship requires something more than some "good ideas we can try out in services." We need a community where those who have authority are open to the contributions of the entire group and where members maintain respect for one another even when disagreeing. Worship reform is inextricably related to how we live and work together as a church. When people do not trust one another or lack the will to maintain mutual respect through periods of conflict, reform becomes impossible. The energy needed for creative work is then drained away by suspicion and by internal battles to gain self-recognition and to negate the value of others. The reform of worship, like all other reforms, requires a healthy, functioning community in which people sense that they matter, that they will be taken seriously even when the group decides not to use their ideas.

A major ingredient in building such a community is a clear understanding of what people's roles are in developing and supporting the worship life of a congregation. Unfortunately, people have become suspicious of roles: "These conventions, now condemned as constricting, artificial, and deadening to emotional spontaneity, formerly established civilized boundaries between people, set limits on the public display of feeling, and promoted cosmopolitanism and civility."[1] Popular culture stresses knowing the real person instead of the role someone fills. A television interview is called "Up Close and Personal," and a national magazine is named *People*. This contemporary cultural perspective often pervades our church meetings and is sometimes amplified by the mistaken notion that being Christian means sharing whatever one feels. To take this hyper-personalized approach to the worship life of a congregation spells disaster. Of course, what people believe, think, and feel matters. We hope our ten-step process in the chapter "Soar with the Wind" has made that clear. However, the best way to guarantee that the congregation's faith and life are adequately expressed in its services is to help people understand both the limits and the functions of their roles in worship.

Sometimes people violate those limits: ministers may act as if the service is their show to be designed and carried out exactly as they wish; musicians may make selections purely on the basis of their artistic biases; lay people may threaten never to come back and to withdraw their support if something is or is not done a certain way. In every case it is a matter of people exploiting their roles, using their particular positions in the community to force their wills upon the congregation.

A positive understanding of our role is one in which we see that the church has granted us a responsibility on behalf of the entire congregation. We have been entrusted with power not to do whatever we want, but to help the church use all of its gifts in the praise of God.

Sometimes people act destructively because no one has made it clear that they have a positive role to fill. For example, if lay people do not realize that it is their role to provide helpful critical response to the worship leadership, they may mutter their complaints privately but never publicly. When the gossip finally gets back to the leaders, it tends to make them defensive and resentful. How much better it is for the community's life when congregation members know that their role includes affirming what is strong and identifying what is weak in the church's worship.

This critical function, however, has its limits. It is not a license to demand what I want or think. It requires a willingness to accept the authority that the community has granted the leaders and an openness to recover lost treasures from the cloud and to try new ways of soaring with the wind. After all, those represent ways of growing in faith, of living up to our promise of discipleship.

Ministers frequently will speak during conferences with affection about some lay person who "keeps me honest, praising me when I do well and leveling with me when things are not going as they should." Congregation members who deal this way with ministers, musicians, and other leaders are performing two vital tasks at once. They are helping the leaders to refine their skills so that they are more effective in their roles, and they are contributing to the community's health by giving the leaders an accurate picture of what is happening in the congregation.

But lay people cannot carry out their role if the leaders are closed to the critical response of the congregation. "I am the one who's had the music training. I should be the one to make the decisions about music." "I am the minister, and this is how we are going to do it." Part of the professional roles of both musicians and ministers is to receive the community's responses and suggestions and to evaluate them, not simply on the basis of personal feelings but in light of the larger truth which comes to us from Scripture, the cloud of witnesses, and the contemporary movement of the Spirit. If the leaders fall into the trap of taking all criticism personally, they will tend to abandon their roles and react simply out of defensiveness and private opinion.

Whenever ministers are tempted to do this, it may be helpful to recall their ordination vows. Although each tradition has its unique perspective, there is one understanding common to all the denominations with which we work: ordination is an act of the church, not the individual who receives it. The community of faith sets the standards, judges if an individual meets them, and defines what the nature of the ministerial role is. Any candidate seeking ordination is keenly aware of this! However, as the years pass after ordination, it is only human to grow accustomed to what was once sought as a distant goal and to blur the lines between one's personal identity and the sacred office. When this happens, ministers can easily assume a pattern of using for their own ends the authority that was granted to them by the community for the community.

The role of worship leaders is not "to do their own thing," but to engage the entire congregation in the praise and service of God. Leaders need to bring strong personal faith and creative vision to their roles; that is part of providing good leadership. But these individual gifts are to be at the service of the church's corporate life. In ordination, the community of faith says, "We confer this role upon you not to escape our responsibility for the church's ministry but in order to help us fulfill our calling. Worship is the work of all God's people; but like every social group that has ever existed, we need a leader to help us do our job as well as we possibly can. We are aching and yearning with all that we are to worship God together as a community. Your role is not to pray and to sing and to praise God for us, but to help us release that prayer which is already in our hearts, that adoration which even now is humming in our bones."

Musicians who lead the congregation's sung praise and prayer may or may not be ordained. The Old Testament describes the leaders of music as a group of people clearly defined by blood line, living in the temple itself, and supported by the institution so that they did not have to assume other work in order to maintain their families: "Now these are the singers, the heads of ancestral houses of the Levites, living in the chambers of the temple free from other service, for they were on duty day and night" (1 Chronicles 9:33).

New Testament singing in corporate worship was largely spontaneous at first, but later, as the community accumulated its valued hymns and songs, the need for management and perpetuation through education of the new Christians fell to those particularly gifted in music. From the fourth century until the Protestant Reformation, the church's music was developed and maintained by the clergy, who were trained in its principles and whose daily liturgies were sung in community.

However, ordination today—with a few outstanding exceptions—is not normally conferred on the basis of musical gifts. Although the gospel is communicated by many means and people are often moved to grasp God's truth through music and art, it is the mastery of the spoken and written Word which is most central to qualification for ordination. Can the candidate preach? Can this person understand and teach the Scriptures? When individuals feel called to lead the church in worship through music, they usually are left to make their own private covenant with God. This affects the church in many ways. Since musicians are not required by an examining board to fit any specific pattern and since they are not granted the privilege of ordination, the importance of their ministry frequently goes unrecognized. Because musicians usually depend on another job as their major source of income, their role is defined as part-time. Even if they have studied organ or choral techniques privately or graduated from a music conservatory, their part-time status restricts their opportunity to improve skills through continuing education and, in many cases, to invest time in practicing their demanding art. All of these factors together tend to keep the musician in the shadows.

The partnership of language, music, and art in worship resembles a wheel in motion. If it is balanced, it carries its load smoothly and picks up momentum easily; but if it is heavy on one side, the ride is bumpy and unstable. When the musician is a permanent member of the worship committee, then the proper balance of all the liturgical elements can be considered from the beginning of the planning process. Whether ordained or not ordained, inexperienced or expert, full-time or part-time, the musician has a vital role to play in engaging the congregation in the praise of God, and that role needs to be adequately recognized if someone is to fill it with grace and enthusiasm.

The Interrelationship of Roles

How lay people, musician, and minister interrelate determines the quality of a church's worship life. If the musician and the pastor treat their roles as sovereign territory, and if the church members fail to express themselves openly, worship reform will fail. Having a clear sense of role does not mean jealously guarding it from the contributions of others. The musician may be gifted with a fine pastoral sensitivity and have excellent ideas about the nonmusical elements in the service. The lay people may be able to identify theological and community issues that need to be integrated into the services. The pastor may have suggestions about musical selections that can strengthen the church's worship. If each listens to the other without feeling threatened, worship reform may become a means of building a mature community of faith. Seen in this light, worship reform is not a goal that we achieve once and for all, then leave behind as we tackle new projects. Instead, it is a means of discipleship. It is one of the major ways in which a congregation lives—not just talks about—justice, trust, respect, and love. It is easy to say we believe in these realities and then deny our faith with a cheap put-down of someone's suggestion or by failing to consult with a colleague or by complaining behind somebody's back or by acting during worship in a way that shows we consider only our own contributions significant. We think here of services in which the minister gets preoccupied looking through notes during the anthem or the musician is seen reading a book during the sermon. How different the effect when the leaders demonstrate a lively interest in every contribution to the worship of God! When the minister sings the hymns enthusiastically, it is greater encouragement for congregational singing than any announcements about increasing participation. When the musician is attentive to every part of the service, he or she provides a worthy model for the choir and congregation.

Worship reform, then, means far more than the introduction of new liturgical practices. It includes constant attentiveness to how we fill our roles and function together as the body of Christ.

The Role of Worship in the Cause of Justice

People sometimes wonder in our workshops if the energy used to reform worship will not drain away a church's impetus for mission in the world. We believe that there is no way the church's witness for justice beyond its walls will be convincing if there is no justice within its walls. A church that lives the gospel in its worship will live the gospel in the world. The two cannot be separated. If we want to deal with the just use of power in economics and politics, then we must exercise power justly in the church. Ministers, musicians, and congregation members who use their roles autocratically in worship do not make effective witnesses for justice in the world.

Our words as well as our actions are significant. How we speak about God and human beings during a service has a profound impact on the way worshipers see themselves and others. The language of worship articulates sacred truth, and, therefore, it is vital for our speech in worship to express the values of God's kingdom and not the prejudices and injustices of the world. For example, throughout this book we have tried to avoid language which excludes people on the basis of gender—such as using the term "man" when we mean women, children, and men. Many people consider this an inconsequential matter when they first hear about it. They often ask, "What is all the fuss? It's just words." But words are never "just words." Words have power. If they did not, we would never bother to read the Bible or listen to a sermon or say a prayer. Words can actually shape our entire perspective on life. Think of the person who was always put down as a child or of someone who was often fed with words of love and encouragement. What a difference those words made! And because worship brings us into the presence of the holy, the power of words is amplified. If our liturgical language raises up one sex, race, nation, or group above others, then the gospel claim that God loves and seeks all people will be denied.

Inclusive language—language that embraces the entire human family—is an integral part of our effort to worship as a community in which "there is no longer Jew or Greek, there is no longer slave or free, there is no longer male and female; for [we] all . . . are one in Christ Jesus" (Galatians 3:28).

But inclusive language alone is not enough. We know how difficult it is for churches to accept the leadership of women. We have seen it with our women seminary graduates. Churches are much more reluctant to accept women than men into positions of power and authority. People feel something "different" when women lead worship. Naturally! That follows from our understanding that worship is never simply ideas which float through our heads. Worship is embodied action that engages all of who we are. Therefore, putting women into leadership roles in worship is bound to have an impact on the congregation's response.

Chapter one of Genesis makes clear that the image of God embraces male and female alike.[2] However, our tradition of male worship leadership has symbolized the masculine at the expense of the feminine. Part of our resistance to women is our anxiety about what their leadership means for the implicit images of God which our tradition has planted in us. If we acknowledge our anxiety and realize that we are being invited not to give up God but to know more completely who God is, then we may be able to move beyond our fear to a fuller relationship with the

Divine. Accepting the worship leadership of women is a way of becoming more open to glory.

In our ministry we have experienced how the power of God moves even more effectively through women and men working together than when they work apart. Each of us initially led worship workshops on our own. Although as individuals we were able to help churches begin reforming their worship, we soon discovered that we could vastly increase the amount of change by providing team leadership to conferences. Participants made clear what was happening in their evaluations: each of us was no longer just talking about women and men, musicians and ministers working together. We were living our principles. We were embodying the realities that before we had only been describing. People sensed that the partnership and the cooperative process which we were teaching are not impossible ideas. They are ways of demonstrating to the church and to the world the justice which God requires from all of us.

The Ultimate Source of All Reform

Our experience of joint ministry has been that it takes a great deal of energy from both of us, but when it works—when we finally soar with the wind—it is not our doing. It is an experience of grace, of being taken over by the truth that is larger than our private worlds. At the end of a worship service or conference our feeling is always more than "We did well." We find ourselves amazed at how God has used our earthbound efforts in ways that we could never have imagined. We return to our separate homes singing in our hearts, "All glory be to God."

What we are describing here is not something that lies down on paper very well. How do you typeset the Spirit? How do you close the wind between the covers of a book? Yet more than anything else it is the Spirit, the vitalizing force of God among us, that we have been writing about in these pages. We have often turned from prose to poetry; we have asked you to step into Rembrandt's picture; we have invoked the heavenly cloud of witnesses; we have stirred up the sounds of instruments and singers; we have pictured people dancing and swaying—all as a way of pointing to that Reality who is greater and more fluent than our most eloquent speech.

We have wanted to provide you with patterns and principles without giving the impression that they are formulas. For the revitalization of worship proceeds not from faith in our methods but from faith in God. Because we believe that "for God all things are possible" (Mark 10:27b), we are released from the assumption of defeat which paralyzes many efforts at reform before they have begun. To assume "It won't work here" is to assume that God is not as great as we claim God is. It is to forget that from a purely human perspective every great act of redemption in the Bible appears as though "It won't work here"—Moses leading the Hebrews through the Red Sea, the settlement of the Promised Land, Christ's resurrection, the spread of the gospel by a tiny band of disciples. Biblical faith is a witness to the fact that the possibilities for life are far greater than what we think them to be. There are unexpected wonders waiting for your congregation that will never be known unless the assumption of predetermined failure is suspended and you trust the Spirit to move through the community in creative ways.

At the start of our ministry together we did not foresee all the experiences and insights we have recorded in this book. One day we sat down over coffee and talked about creating a service that would trace the Protestant Reformation through hymns. We had no idea that poems, music, drama, dance, workshops, and these pages would over the years flow out of that initial conversation. And we have no idea exactly what will flow out of your efforts. But if you trust God for whom all things are possible and if you maintain a community of mutual respect and love, then when you gather to worship, you may sense with joy that though the kingdom of God has not yet come, it is on its way!

Notes

Chapter 1

[1]Walker Percy, *The Second Coming* (New York: Farrar, Straus & Giroux Inc., 1980), p. 159.

[2]Peter L. Berger, *The Sacred Canopy* (New York: Doubleday & Co. Inc., 1969).

[3]Max Frisch, *Man in the Holocene* (New York: Harcourt Brace Jovanovich Inc. 1981).

[4]For an incisive summary of how the church's worship has spoken to changing pastoral needs over the centuries see William H. Willimon, *Worship As Pastoral Care* (Nashville: Abingdon Press, 1979), chapter 2, pp. 31-52.

Chapter 2

[1]This etching appears in A. Hyatt Mayor, *Rembrandt and the Bible* (New York: The Metropolitan Museum of Art, 1979), p. 25. The picture is reproduced by permission of The Metropolitan Museum of Art. Bequest of Mrs. H. O. Havemeyer, 1929. The H. O. Havemeyer Collection (29. 107. 18).

If you would like to reproduce this picture or others for your church's worship, you should: (1) Purchase the book. (2) Write the Permissions Department of the Metropolitan Museum of Art (Fifth Ave. & 82d St., New York, NY 10028), giving the book title, page number, name of the print, and the number of copies you will make. For a modest fee you will receive a photograph suitable for printing.

[2]Poem copyrighted 1982 by Thomas H. Troeger.

[3]Poem copyrighted 1982 by Thomas H. Troeger.

[4]I am indebted to conferees at the College of Preachers and to Leo Malania for the dramatic idea that the father's heart would change when he heard his dead son was now alive.

[5]Poem copyrighted 1982 by Thomas H. Troeger.

[6]Doug Adams, *Meeting House to Camp Meeting* (Austin: The Sharing Company, 1981), pp. 48-49.

[7]William H. Willimon, *Worship As Pastoral Care* (Nashville: Abingdon Press, 1979), p. 162.

[8]Poem copyrighted 1982 by Thomas H. Troeger.

[9]John Smyth, "The Differences of the Churches of the Seperation . . ." (1608), republished in *The Works of John Smyth* (Cambridge: Cambridge University Press, 1915), p. 277.

[10]T. S. Eliot, "Burnt Norton," *Four Quartets* (New York: Harcourt Brace Jovanovich Inc.; London: Faber and Faber Ltd., 1952), p. 121.

[11]Robert Frost, "Mending Wall," in *The Poetry of Robert Frost*. Edited by Edward Connery Latham (New York: Holt, Rinehart and Winston, 1975), p. 34.

[12]Willy Malacher, "Process Toward Design," in *Liturgy* magazine, vol. 23, no. 5 (September, 1978), p. 31.

Chapter 3

[1]"Prayer to Every God," in James B. Pritchard, ed., *Ancient Near Eastern Texts* . . . (Princeton: Princeton University Press, 1969), pp. 391-392.

[2]Czeslaw Milosz, *Native Realm: A Search for Self-Definition* (New York: Doubleday & Co. Inc., 1968), p. 83.

[3]Walt Whitman, "To Think of Time," in Oscar Williams, ed., *A Pocket Book of Modern Verse* (New York: Washington Square Press, 1962), p. 27.

[4]For a concise, highly readable introduction to how worship has changed over the years, see William H. Willimon, *Word, Water, Wine and Bread* (Valley Forge: Judson Press, 1980).

[5]Herbert G. May and Bruce M. Metzger, eds., *The New Oxford Annotated Bible* (New York: Oxford University Press, 1973), p. 488.

[6]Hans-Joachim Kraus, *Worship in Israel: A Cultic History of Old Testament* (Richmond, Va.: John Knox Press, 1966), p. 197. Copyright Basil Blackwell, 1966. Used by permission.

[7]*Ibid.*, p. 201.

[8]*Ibid.*, p. 203.

[9]We are indebted to a former colleague, Richard L. Manzelmann, for first clarifying these first two points.

[10]H. H. Rowley, *Worship in Ancient Israel* (Philadelphia: Fortress Press, 1967), p. 39.

[11]Eusebius, "Ecclesiastical History" III. 39, in Henry Bettenson, ed., *Documents of the Christian Church* (New York: Oxford University Press, 1947), p. 39.

[12]Frank Kermode, *The Genesis of Secrecy* (Cambridge, Mass.: Harvard University Press, 1979), p. 17.

[13]*Ibid.*, p. 17.

[14]D. M. Thomas, *The White Hotel* (New York: The Viking Press, 1981), pp. 257-274.

[15] Willimon, *Word, Water, Wine and Bread*, p. 25.

[16] "The First Apology of Justin Martyr," in Bard Thompson, ed., *Liturgies of the Western Church* (Cleveland and New York: The William Collins + World Publishing Company, 1975), p. 8.

[17] "The Apostolic Tradition of Hippolytus," in *ibid.*, p. 21.

[18] *Ibid.*, p. 22.

[19] The word "hymn" means the text we sing. The melody is the "hymn tune."

[20] A chord is the sound of several tones played or sung at the same time—the harmony. Melody is a succession of single tones one after another. In the chorales, the top notes of successive chords form the melody.

[21] Louis Benson, *The English Hymn* (Richmond, Va.: John Knox Press, 1915), pp. 293-294.

[22] John Spencer Curwen, *Studies in Worship Music*, 2nd Series (London: J. Curwen & Sons, 1885), pp. 39-40.

[23] Erik Routley, *The Music of Christian Hymns* (Chicago: G. I. A. Publications, Inc., 1981), p. 21.

[24] Ulrich S. Leupold, ed.; Helmut T. Lehmann, general ed., *Luther's Works*, Volume 53—Liturgy and Hymns (Philadelphia: Fortress Press, 1965), p. 149.

[25] *The Book of Common Prayer* (New York: The Church Hymnal Corporation and The Seabury Press Inc., 1979), p. 331.

[26] Oscar Cullman, *Early Christian Worship* (Chicago: Henry Regnery Company, 1953), pp. 32-33.

[27] Raymond E. Brown, *The Birth of the Messiah* (New York: Doubleday & Co. Inc., 1979), pp. 350-355.

[28] Dom Gregory Dix, *The Shape of the Liturgy* (Westminster: Dacre Press, 1943), p. 436.

[29] Richard M. Spielmann, *History of Christian Worship* (New York: The Seabury Press Inc., 1969), p. 40.

[30] Irah Chase, trans., *The Constitutions of the Holy Apostles* (New York: D. Appleton & Company, 1847), p. 69.

[31] John Russell, "A Collector's Stained Glass Goes on View at Cloisters," in *The New York Times*, February 26, 1982, p. C 18.

[32] Spielmann, *op. cit.*, p. 59.

[33] J. G. Davies, ed., *The Westminister Dictionary of Worship* (Philadelphia: The Westminster Press, 1976), pp. 28-29.

[34] Thompson, *op. cit.*, p. 104.

[35] *Ibid.*, p. 190.

[36] Spielmann, *op. cit.*, pp. 110-111.

[37] "The Second Act of Uniformity," quoted by Dix, *op. cit.*, p. 658.

[38] John Smyth, "The Differences of the Churches of the Seperation . . ." (1608), republished *The Works of John Smyth* (Cambridge: Cambridge University Press, 1915), p. 271.

[39] D. Mervyn Himbury, *British Baptists: A Short History* (London: The Carey Kingsgate Press Limited, 1962), p. 7.

[40] *The Works of John Smyth*, pp. lxx-lxxi. The precise date of this letter is not known. The cursive has faded and when I examined it in April, 1982, in the British Museum, I could not discern the date.

[41] *Ibid.*, p. 277.

[42] *Ibid.*, p. 271.

[43] *Ibid.*, p. 272.

[44] Bettenson, *op. cit.*, p. 353.

[45]Doug Adams, *Meeting House to Camp Meeting* (Austin: The Sharing Company, 1981), p. 13.

[46]John E. Skoglund, *Worship in the Free Churches* (Valley Forge: The Judson Press, 1965), pp. 15-17.

[47]Adams, *op. cit.*, p. 15.

[48]We are indebted here to Urban T. Holmes III, *Ministry and Imagination* (New York: The Seabury Press Inc., 1976), especially chapter 5, pp. 111-136.

[49]Dix, *op. cit.*, p. 658.

[50]H. Barry Evans, ed., *Prayer Book Renewal* (New York: The Seabury Press Inc., 1978), p. 6.

Chapter 4

[1]Thomas H. Troeger, *Word and Witness*, Preaching Service (5/20/82) Sunday Publications, Lake Worth, Florida.

[2]Dom Gregory Dix, *The Shape of the Liturgy* (Westminster: Dacre Press, 1943), p. 12.

[3]John Donne, "Devotions upon Emergent Occasions," in Charles M. Coffin, ed., *The Complete Poetry and Selected Prose of John Donne* (New York: The Modern Library, 1952), p. 446.

[4]David Macaulay, *Cathedral* (Boston: Houghton Mifflin Co., 1973), the preface.

[5]Poem copyrighted 1982 by Thomas H. Troeger.

[6]Poem copyrighted 1982 by Thomas H. Troeger.

[7]J. G. Davies, *The Westminster Dictionary of Worship* (Philadelphia: The Westminster Press, 1976), pp. 315-318. This is a wonderfully useful reference book for worship leaders.

[8]Leonard Ellinwood, *The History of American Church Music* (New York: Da Capo Press Inc., 1970), p. 41.

Chapter 5

[1]James Dittes, *When the People Say No* (San Francisco: Harper & Row, Publishers Inc., 1979), p. 4.

[2]Poem copyrighted 1982 by Thomas Troeger.

Chapter 6

[1]Anna Kisselgoff, an interview in *The New York Times*, April 27, 1978, p. C 16.

[2]*Ibid.*, p. C 16.

[3]This was made possible by a grant from the Luce Foundation. However, a local congregation or a group of churches could hire a professional dancer for a limited number of sessions. If you do this, make clear what your goal is: not to become professional dancers yourselves but to learn simple ways of walking, standing, and moving that express your faith more completely.

[4]John Bunyan, *The Pilgrim's Progress*, arranged for the modern reader by E. W. Walters (Nashville: Cokesbury Press, 1938), p. 30.

[5]I am indebted to a sermon by Joan Delaplane for suggesting this exercise and inspiring the subsequent poem.

[6]Poem copyrighted 1982 by Thomas H. Troeger.

Chapter 7

[1]Christopher Lasch, *The Culture of Narcissism* (New York: Warner Books Inc., 1979), p. 65.

[2]For a sophisticated yet lucid discussion of this topic see Phyllis Trible, *God and the Rhetoric of Sexuality* (Philadelphia: Fortress Press, 1978), pp. 12-23.